The American Men of Letters Series

The American Men of Letters Series

Theodore Dreiser, 1943

Theodore Dreiser

F. O. Matthiessen

The American Men of Letters Series

GREENWOOD PRESS, PUBLISHERS
WESTPORT, CONNECTICUT

The Library of Congress has catalogued this publication as follows:

Library of Congress Cataloging in Publication Data

Matthiessen, Francis Otto, 1902-1950.
   Theodore Dreiser.

   Original ed. issued in series: The American men
of letters.
   Includes bibliographical references.
   1. Dreiser, Theodore, 1871-1945. I. Series:
The American men of letters series.
PS3507.R55Z7 1973   813'.5'2 [B]   72-7876
ISBN 0-8371-6550-4

The chapter "Of Crime and Punishment" originally appeared in *Monthly Review*, October 1950, Copyright 1950 by *Monthly Review*.

Typography and format designed by
LEONARD W. BLIZARD

Contents

Editors' Note

THE AUTHOR of this work had completed it before his death but had not revised it beyond the point of penciling many alterations and corrections in the manuscript, the last two chapters of which were in his own handwriting. The editors of the American Men of Letters Series were so well satisfied, however, with the biography as it stood that they proceeded with its publication in the faith that it not only expressed the main intention of its writer but was a moving and illuminating treatment of Theodore Dreiser and his times. In that faith they present it without other changes than those necessary to prepare the manuscript for the printer.

Theodore Dreiser

An Indiana Boyhood

THEODORE DREISER has left us his own picture of his childhood and youth. A writer's account of his experiences may not square at all points with the facts, but it is the kind of reality in which the novelist deals, his image of essential life. In Dreiser's first drafts for the two vast volumes, running to half a million words, which took him only up to his arrival in New York at twenty-three, he called this work *A Book about Myself*. It was characteristic of his imagination to make no sharp separation between document and fiction. This is not to say that he took liberties with the record, though he was acutely conscious of how hard it was to tell the truth, especially about his own character, and he believed he could succeed only by immense detail. He shocked some respectable reviewers into denouncing him as shameless for the fullness with which he recounted an act of stealing. But he refused to leave anything out, no matter how unflattering to himself.

Yet he did not lose sight of the main significant contours. He cited Nietzsche's belief that we all have our typical experiences. Nearly everything most typical of Dreiser's inner nature might be suggested through his early contrasting feelings for his parents: his attraction to his mother, his repulsion from his father. He shared nevertheless in qualities inherited from them both: in his mother's emotional warmth and openness to life, in his father's dogged tenacity.

John Paul Dreiser was a German and, in his son's estimate, a Catholic bigot. At all events he was doubly an outsider in an America that was still basically Anglo-Saxon and that was already drifting away from any strict patterns of theological dogma. The theme of the outsider, though of a different sort, is the most recurrent in Dreiser's work. He knew what it meant from his earliest memories, from when he had hung around the railroad tracks in Terre Haute, helping his older brothers and sisters pick up the scattered bits of coal that were desperately needed for the family fire. He was the poor boy staring hungrily into the bright windows of the rich. He was himself to be caught for a time by the American dream of material success. It would hardly have occurred to him that he was destined to break through in a different sphere, as virtually the first major American writer whose family name was not English or Scotch Irish. Whitman and Melville, to be sure, were Dutch on their mother's side, but Thoreau came by a French name only through the Channel Islands. Dreiser's own immediate contemporaries, Crane and Norris, were still as basically English in their forebears as Howells and Clemens. Only with the generation after Dreiser did our cultural life begin to reflect the more complex mixture that we have become.

Dreiser's father was born at Mayen on the Moselle, fifteen miles from Coblentz. He had left there to escape con-

scription, and in 1844, after a short time in France, he had
set out for America, at twenty-three, to make his fortune.
He was a weaver by trade, and gradually worked his way
west from New York, supporting himself along the way as
a peddler. By the mid-century he was connected with a
woolen mill at Dayton, Ohio. In the countryside nearby
he had met and fallen in love with Sarah Schanab, the
daughter of a prospering Moravian farmer. The Schanabs
were Mennonites by faith, and Sarah's father was opposed
to her marrying a Catholic. But she eloped with John Paul
at sixteen.

He was industrious and on his way up. The couple soon
moved farther west, to Fort Wayne, Indiana, where John
Paul became a production manager. He had presently
raised enough money to build a mill of his own at Sullivan,
a small town on the southwest margin of the state. The mill
did well for a time, and though the first three children had
died, eight more were born during the dozen years before
1870.

Then the mill burned, uninsured. As he tried to gain his
footing again, after being seriously injured by a falling
beam during the job of rebuilding, he was cheated by what
the family called the "Yankee trickery" of strangers, and he
lost all the remainder of his property. His dream of wealth
ended there. He began to withdraw into himself, and tried
to discipline his children into severe religious behavior. He
was a broken-spirited man of fifty when his son Theodore
was born on Ninth Street in Terre Haute on August 27,
1871.

During the first six years of Dreiser's life, his father
had no steady job. When a mill shut down for the winter,
he would take whatever he could get. He no longer pos-

sessed courage or initiative. Yet he clung to his strict conception of the role played by the head of the family—a practice which, as his son noted, "did not flourish in this looser western social polity." Tension mounted between him and his older children, "who, because of long suffering at his critical hands, and because of the practical contributions they were making from time to time toward the support of the home, were no longer prepared to listen, much less to accept, his diatribes on conduct." In full reaction against his orthodox moralism, they were "caught fast by the material, unreligious aspect of things." It did him no good to grow violent in his denunciations of his daughters as they began to walk out with boys in the evenings.

The chief childhood image that Dreiser kept of his father was of "a thin grasshopper of a man, brooding wearily," his reddish beard resting on his chest as he sat with the Lives of the Saints or a German newspaper on his lap. In retrospect Dreiser was not "really bitter" towards his narrowness. Yet this father possessed no warmth to draw his children to him. He was an image of authority to be obeyed when necessary, but not respected. He seems to have noted that Theodore was endowed with "an abnormally inquiring mind." But this son was to come to the conclusion that his father had no real knowledge of life, that he took it to be "not what it is, but what it is said to be, or written to be, by others." What this son held against him longest was his unalterable insistence that his children attend the poorly equipped parochial schools. Dreiser believed that this prevented all of them from acquiring any adequate education. In his own case the German priests conveyed to him no more of their faith than a threat of grim punishments which numbed him with fear. This image of authority, a further projection of his father, was one that could only be rejected.

He described himself as "always a 'mother child.'" One of the earliest memories he recalled of her presence was of sitting on the floor stroking her feet. "I can hear her now. 'See poor mother's shoes? Aren't you sorry she has to wear such torn shoes? See the hole here.' She reached down to show me, and in wonder, and finally pity—evoked by the tone of her voice which so long controlled me—I began to examine, growing more and more sorrowful as I did so. And then, finally, a sudden swelling sense of pity that ended in tears. I smoothed her shoes and cried. I recall her taking me up and holding me affectionately against her breast and smoothing my head. Then feeling still more sorrowful and helpless, I presume, I cried the more. But that was the birth of sympathy and tenderness in me."

Dreiser was to be intensely conscious of the "newness" of his world, of the first time he saw a telephone and an electric light, of the first trolley cars that were being put on the streets of Chicago by Charles T. Yerkes just as Dreiser, as a boy in his teens, was beginning to try his luck in the city. Unlike Sherwood Anderson, who preserved loving images of the Middle Western country life before the industrial machines had broken its slower rhythms, Dreiser was nearly always to find his subjects in the new big cities. It was largely due to his mother that he kept any awareness of an older America, through hearing her speak "of her parents' prosperity as farmers, of orchard and meadow and great fields of grain, and of some of the primitive conditions and devices of pioneer life that still affected them—neighbors borrowing fire, Indians coming to the door to beg or be sociable, the spinning of wool and cotton on hand looms, the home manufacture of soap, shoes, and furniture." Behind this picture of her girlhood lay the dim background of her Czech forebears in Moravia, of her family name which, in accordance with the bewildered American way of dealing with foreign sounds, was presently altered from Schanab to Snepp.

Her nature was opposite to her husband's in being basically unmoral. She took the view that human beings had trouble enough maintaining themselves without being harried further by social or religious opinion. Dreiser wrote many passages of loving tribute to her, swelling into rhythms of a Whitman-like amplitude in order to reach her emotional generosity and placidness, in which, incidentally, she seems to have been very like Whitman's mother. She was never "mentally incisive," and it was not until Theodore could help her, after his own first years at school, that she finally learned how to write. But she was "a temperament to be reckoned with: strong, patient, understanding, sympathetic, creative, humor-loving, and helpful. . . . A magnetic dreamy soul . . . beyond or behind so-called good and evil. . . . A happy, hopeful, animal mother, with a desire to live, and not much constructive ability wherewith to make real her dreams."

But she lived very richly through her many children, with all their affairs and problems enfolded in her embrace. Their responding love for her was based upon her faith in and enthusiasm for them. She gave them constant encouragement, out of the depths of her often "all too tired courage." Dorsch, as the family sometimes called him, also remembered her "round-faced delight" when some of them came home with money. Hanging about his five older sisters, it always seemed to him that "no one ever wanted me *enough,* unless it was my mother." Then he added, with characteristic honesty: "Later there were those who wanted me too much, and where I did not 'want'!"

Only once did she sink into "a dumb despair." This was when she was first confronted with their time of worst poverty. It began after the panic of 1877, with an "unbroken stretch of privation and misery . . . a dour and despondent period which seems to have colored my life forever." His father was out of work altogether for more than a year. His earnest anxious mind deemed the family disgraced when they could not meet their bills, and he sometimes harbored ill-feeling for what he considered his wife's slacker ways. This was the time when Theodore learned to steal coal.

They had moved several times within Terre Haute, to poorer and poorer houses. But now they had to face the fact that the family must break up. The father was to try whatever city seemed most likely to offer work, the older children were to strike out variously on their own, and the mother was to take the three youngest—Tillie, Theodore, and Edward (born two years after Theodore)—to a smaller town where living would be cheaper.

They first tried nearby Vincennes, a French-American town, where Dreiser's mother knew the fire chief's wife, who had previously been a seamstress in Terre Haute and who now offered to put them up over the fire house. This stay ended abruptly a few weeks later when Mrs. Dreiser discovered to her consternation that another part of the same quarters served as a brothel. But they did not leave before Theodore had caught an awed glimpse, through a half-open door, of "a corn-haired blonde, her pink face buried in a curled arm, lying on a bed allotted to one of the firemen serving on the night shift."

They then went back to Sullivan. Dreiser was to remember his three years there, between his seventh and tenth birthdays, as perhaps the happiest of his life. "Infancy and its complete non-understanding had just gone . . . adolescence had not yet arrived." Their stay in a plain little white house in "dirty old" Sullivan was compounded most for him "of innocence, wonder, beauty." Yet their poverty was still at its worst, They moved in with only a couple of straw-filled mattresses, three or four quilts and a wooden chair, an iron cooking pot, a few borrowed plates and pans, no table and no stove. Theodore and Ed had no shoes to wear to school, and were sent home as the only boys without them. Their mother took in boarders and did washing or whatever other work was available.

As the home became established, the other children began to drift back for longer or shorter stays, particularly the four older sisters—Mame, Emma, Theresa, and Sylvia—and Theodore's next oldest brother, Alphonse Joachim or Al, who had been sent to help on a cousin's farm in the northern part of the state. Their father came too on brief occasions, though "gloomy and depressed" at being in no position "to put right his disordered affairs." Yet, in spite of everything, Dreiser felt this home "full of a kind of sweetness that never since has anywhere been equalled for me." In his mother's presence, no matter what deprivations, life always seemed "radiant."

Here in Sullivan he was "vibrating with an emotional ecstasy at the spectacle of life itself. The lower Wabash valley was a "lush Egyptian land . . . drowsy with heat in summer." He began to develop "a delicious sense of wonder and delight" in nature itself, as he followed with curiosity the flights of birds, or went foraging for corn. The boardinghouse his mother kept was not exactly the quiet orderly realm which Howells believed to be one of the most characteristic milieus for American fiction. Among the various seasonal workers who put up there, was a giant of a man who loved to show the boys card tricks, but threatened with a knife when he was drunk, and was presently found to be wanted for murder. Dreiser was to feel that he had been unusually lucky in the richness of human material that had poured upon his consciousness from the start. Here in Sullivan, too, the death of an old man in the shabby house next door gave him his first suggestion "of the paltry import of our individual lives." There was not even money enough to pay for a funeral, and once again Theodore experienced the oppressive physical dread of poverty and defeat which remained ingrained in him for life.

One day his brother Paul turned up, after an absence of several years. He was the oldest, thirteen years Theodore's senior, and during their bad times in Terre Haute he had forged a note and gone to jail. Their father had wanted him to study for the priesthood; but, in the mood of revolt common to the family, he had broken away and begun to find his talents as an end-man and song-writer for a strolling minstrel troupe promoting Hamlin's Wizard Oil. By the date of his return he was already the author of *The Paul Dresser Songster*—his name had seemed easier this way to the Middle Western tongue—and now, very grand in a fur coat and silk hat, he had come back to help his mother. He had her warm gray-blue eyes and much of her emotional generosity. Paul thought they would all be better off at Evansville, in the southernmost part of the state, where (unbeknownst to his mother) his mistress—the original of "My Gal Sal"—was a madam. He helped establish them there in a cottage rented from her.

By then the older girls, wistful and eager but also "restless, determined, half-educated," were stirring up comment when they strolled the streets, made up with "spit curls" and rouge. One of them had already been seduced by a prominent lawyer and office-holder in Terre Haute. But this was the same man who had volunteered to get Paul out of jail, a circumstance which taught Dreiser early that there is no easy separation into evil and good.

The only member of the family who went wholly to the bad was the second brother, Marcus Romanus or Rome. He was the only one who was really selfish, who thought that "the world was made for him, not he for it." After an early job selling candy and magazines on a train, he took to the road for adventures, and would send back postcards from Cheyenne or Duluth: "All right with me. Don't worry. See you Christmas." But his bragging stories of experiences among copper miners or cowboys could not conceal that he was a recklessly unsuccessful gambler and rapidly becoming a victim to drink. His periodic returns home began to be only cycles of disaster: drunkenness, impositions on others, rows with the local police, and fines to be paid by someone else. He would be dead by forty in a South Clark Street dive in Chicago.

Al, four years older than Theodore, was the closest to him and his natural protector in fights for which he had no relish and no skill. These left him shy of other boys, and wondering why life was "so fierce." Al also shared with him half of his schoolboy winnings, since Theodore never seemed to win anything at all. In retrospect Dreiser thought that this brother was "intended to be a better writer than I could ever be," but that his sensitive intelligence had been hopelessly thwarted by lack of education. Al was also the one who suffered most from the economic struggle for survival. He came to feel disheartened and defeated. After they were grown up, these brothers drifted apart. Once Theodore had come on to New York, he lost track of Al altogether.

As Dreiser recognized, this family group was "of a peculiarly nebulous, emotional, unorganized, and traditionless character." But he also believed that a "more genial and affectionate" unit could hardly have been found. At the times when most of them were together, they formed a continual school of experience for him, a "chaffering camp" in which "every theory of living" was discussed. Henry James had used almost the same phrases to characterize his family circle, though the only likeness between these two groups lay in their warmth. Al, for example, thought that as a result of too little money and too little order their family affairs were usually in "an awful botch." Their mother gave them all her devotion, but she had no understanding of management or planning. In each new community they found themselves discredited for not having done well financially. And they were always being isolated by local conventional notions of propriety.

Paul and his mistress quarreled, and the Dreisers had to give up their cottage. Several of the older children had already been drawn to Chicago, and now urged their mother to come. She moved there in the summer when Theodore was not quite thirteen. He was more excited by the violently growing city than by anything in his life so far, but he was also scared by its noise and confusion. His father was there with them, still stubborn and dictatorial in his religious views, but deeply depressed by his inability to cope any longer with the business world. When he was unable to find work of any sort in Chicago—he was now over sixty—their hopes of establishing a home there collapsed. Mrs. Dreiser and the younger children retreated again to Indiana, this time to Warsaw in the lake country to the north, near some of her cousins.

At last he escaped from the parochial school. The one at Evansville had been the poorest of all, and he felt that he had learned really nothing in two years. His mother had had her own doubts about it, but these had been ineffectual before his father's insistence. But now he was allowed to enter the public school, in the seventh grade. His first awakening excitement in study came through his young English teacher, May Calvert, who said: "I can't tell you how beautifully you read, Theodore. It is so natural; you make everything so real." There had been hardly any books in his home, save a stray Catholic story or two, and then Hill's *Manual of Social and Business Forms*, which an agent at the door had persuaded his mother to buy, and which Theodore had discovered to his delight to be interspersed with stories and poems. Through some of the boys he had also made the acquaintance of current Horatio Alger favorites.

But now Miss Calvert opened the door into a whole new world. Irving's *Alhambra* enchanted him with its descriptions of a distant exotic realm. *The Water Babies* made his mind expand with a rush of curiosity about science—a fact which raises the question whether his later strong sense of the mysteries of science may not have been heightened by his having had no contacts with it in his youth. Now every book was a new experience. Samuel Smiles's *Self-Help* quickened in him an eagerness to succeed. Lew Wallace's *Ben-Hur*, which had appeared only a few years before, recommended itself to him as by a great Indiana author. But as he lists in his autobiography the other standard authors whose acquaintance he began to make, the mentions sound a little perfunctory, and another remark is thrown into sharper relief: that he always learned more directly from life itself. His "first introduction to the mystery of form" came through watching a potter in an open window turning his wheel.

The only subject he failed in was grammar, whose rudiments the German priests had never managed to teach him. But even with this deficiency he was promoted to the eighth grade and then into high school, where Miss Mildred Fielding (who had come from Malden, Massachusetts, to be director of the recitation room) became an important influence upon him. In view of his background she urged him to study German, so that he might read Goethe and Heine. Through her tutelage he also picked up his first bits of knowledge of zoology, chemistry, and physics, and became an absorbed reader of history. She commended him to the superintendent for "a description of a local scene." Most important, she told him privately one day that he had a much more sensitive mind than the rest of the class, that he must study to go on, for she knew he would find his way. When she said that, he was moved so close to tears that he could not speak.

He had grown very tall and spindling, and he worried that he must be terribly homely and unattractive. One of his sisters had come home to bear an illegitimate child, and he realized that his thoughts were now continually on girls, as his sisters' were on men. Yet he was excessively shy, even though his body began to feel "driven," as it was to continue to be for the rest of his life. He used the same word that he applied to Cowperwood when he said that he was "blazing" with sex. One early April evening he had his first sudden unexpected and frightening intercourse with the daughter of the baker. But this served only to throw him back into worse timidity, which lasted until he was nearly twenty. As a result he "fell into the ridiculous and unsatisfactory practice of masturbation," and was then racked with morbid anxiety that he had been ruined by it.

But over this span of the years his heart reverted happily to Warsaw, to an idyllic picture of its tall sycamores and fragrant hayfields, its nearby lakes and woods. More than any other place this little town meant his mother to him, for here he "first came partially to understand her, to view her as a woman and to know how remarkable she was. . . . I really adored her." He was to think of her as "pagan" in her hearty earthiness. But he felt himself held strongest by "the silver tether of her affection, understanding, sweetness, sacrifice." These are the qualities that he would weave into his own favorite heroine, Jennie Gerhardt, just as Jennie's old father would be a largely forgiving likeness of his own father's sternness.

In the summer after finishing the first year of high school, he was filled more and more with "a wild flaming enthusiasm for the color of life." But now, at fifteen, he was also "beginning to be caught by the American spirit of material advancement." One day he came in and said: "Ma, I am going to Chicago."

Chicago, Chicago!

THE train trip from Warsaw was the first he had ever made alone, and his excitement on his arrival is what he remembered when writing about Sister Carrie. The great Chicago fire had occurred the year he was born, and the new city for which Louis Sullivan hoped so much was now rising along the lake. This very summer Frank Lloyd Wright had left the University of Wisconsin after his freshman year to go to work in Sullivan's office. Absorbing this master's belief in Walt Whitman's dream of an organic art for American democracy, Wright was to have a career a little like Dreiser's in the lonely intransigence with which he had to fight against the prevailing tameness of taste.

The Haymarket riot had taken place only the year before, but no reverberations of social tension would seem to have reached Dreiser, for whom, as for Carrie, the streetcars were a song. The fortunes of McCormick and Field, Armour and Swift, Gary and Pullman were in full career, and though Dreiser may not yet have known all their names, the sprawling city that their industries were calling into being burned for him with "an electric luster." And when he relived these memories at sixty, his feelings rose into a prose poem to "Working Chicago."

Two of his sisters were living there, one of them now married, and Al had a job in Milwaukee; but Theodore had no intention of being dependent upon any of them, and struck out at once to look for work for himself. But it was not easy to find. He had to get used to the cold refrain, "Nothing to-day," and an undertone of fear began to mingle with his excitement. Eventually he landed a job as a combination dish-washer and busboy for a Greek, in a miserable and filthy place. Then he realized another fact of working conditions: that once in a job, no matter how unsatisfactory, it was very hard to find time to look for something better. It was only when he got sick, and concluded with the same despondency as his first heroine that this meant his job was lost, that he found himself free to start all over again.

He held no flattering view of his capacities. He realized that he must have impressed any employers as "too large, too weak, too nebulous, too dull." He was to describe himself as he described so many of his adolescents in his fiction, as "wistful" and "dreamy": "a shambling, scatterbrained, meaningless and mooning incompetent . . . I needed to cultivate reticence—an observation which still holds true."

The best position he found was as a shipping clerk, at five dollars a week, with Hibbard, Spencer, & Bartlett, a wholesale hardware firm. By then his mother and much of the rest of the family had arrived to try to set up another home. And though his father was with them only because he was unable to find employment, Dreiser concluded of this period that, with nearly all the children contributing some money, "the state of our family as a collective unit at this time was perhaps as good as it ever was, before or after."

He was himself in poor health, suffering from a chronic stomach ailment, and spitting blood from the dust and excelsior which he had to inhale all day. He seems to have suffered even more from not being able to afford any decent clothes—a fact of growing importance to him in the city. But nothing could dim for long the promise that its lights had held out that first night he had put up at a boardinghouse on Madison Street. These lights were like "an Aladdin view in the *Arabian Nights.*" This was to remain one of his favorite phrases for evoking glamor. The city itself was to be etched in his brain in an endless series of pictures of tall new towers silhouetted against the lake, of the black oily river as he hung along its bridges, of the immeasurable energy that pulsated from the grain elevators and railroad yards and the vast central building of the Board of Trade. It seemed to say: "You are part of me, I of you! All that life is or hope is . . . this I am. . . . Live, live, satisfy your heart! Strive to be what you wish to be now while you are young and of it! . . . Be, be, wonderful or strong or great, if you will but be!" Though phrased far more loosely, this is oddly close to what Lambert Strether learned in Paris and James expressed as one of the central themes in his fiction.

But in the two years that Dreiser now worked in the city he hardly seemed destined to vibrate at anything like this pitch. Then followed one of the most remarkable incidents of his career. Miss Fielding, who had become the principal of a school in Chicago, suddenly appeared at the office one day, with her mind made up. He was wasting himself, and he must allow her to arrange for him to go to Indiana University as a special student. She had worked out all the details, had saved up the money, and insisted that he accept it. She must have pondered and yearned over qualities latent in him that he had not begun to suspect for himself. She was firm in her belief that he could make something valuable of his life. He needed to cultivate his mind. "Read Spencer," she said. "Read a life of Socrates. Read Marcus Aurelius and Emerson."

To Dreiser's memory, Miss Fielding was "an old maid, with a set of false upper teeth, and a heavenly, irradiating smile. She had led a very hard life herself, and did not wish me to." Four years later—long before he had begun to realize the full value of what she had done for him, or even to understand why she had done it—she had married and then died in childbirth.

He was never to forget his gratitude to her. Not that his year at college amounted to anything extraordinary in itself. He felt that he was too lacking in exact training, especially in mathematics, to learn "quite what it was all about." But he studied history and philology (as Miss Fielding had urged), literature, and elementary Latin, and was conditioned only in a term of geometry. His horizons expanded most by listening to the other students talk. Yet he was again the outsider, and continually reminded of it. He was not asked to join a fraternity. In meeting girls he was bothered more than ever by his lack of clothes and money. At the end of the year he had a sense that he had wasted it, and that he did not know enough to profit from Miss Fielding's generous offer to let him return for another. Yet this solitary year proved to be one of the "most vitalizing" periods of his life. He learned for the first time what it meant to be "a free intellectual agent." He left with a feeling of inadequacy before the curriculum, and yet with the first glimmering sense of the companionship in knowledge.

This was really his farewell to Indiana, to which he was to return only as a tourist a quarter of a century later. But then he renewed his pleasure in the unpretentious charm of its fertile bottom lands, in the "delicate, poetic, generative" quality in its hazy atmosphere. On that occasion the author of *The Titan* did not call on the author of "Little Orphant Annie," then at the top of his popularity, but only because Dreiser had heard that James Whitcomb Riley "did not approve" of his novels. He found in Riley's poems "a kind of wistfulness that is the natural accompaniment of the dream of unsophistication." It never occurred to him to reject them, even for their crude sentimentality.

Back in Chicago after his year in Bloomington, still with no definite plans for the future, he took a job in a newly opened real-estate office which seemed to promise expansion. Paul, who was now a nationally known figure, and whose song, "I Believe It For My Mother Told Me So," was being sung everywhere that summer, was with them for one of his infrequent but heartening visits. What they all began to notice was that their mother was rapidly failing. She was only in her mid-fifties, but "she had come such a long way in poverty" that her energies seemed exhausted. Theodore wanted to be with her as much as possible, to comfort her out of a new "brooding wistfulness" if he could. Her doctor was not able to make any coherent diagnosis, but she suddenly collapsed and died in Theodore's arms as he was helping her to the stool.

His final rebellion against the Church, which marked the end of his relations with it, arose from the funeral. His

mother, a Catholic only through marriage, had been intermittent in her duties, and the priest whom their father now
called raised the question whether she could be buried in
consecrated ground. Ultimately, she was, but even the rais-
ing of such a question over his blessed mother filled
Dreiser's heart with great bitterness.

The whole experience of her death was "the most profound psychologic shake-up" he ever went through. Al was
the first to sense that this meant the end of their home.
Without their mother's enfolding presence quarrels quickly
broke out among their diverse temperaments, and the three
youngest decided to try an apartment by themselves. When
the moment of leave-taking came, Dreiser was suddenly
struck by how old and frail his father looked. "Well,
you're going, are you? I'm sorry, Dorsch. I done the best I
could. The girls, they won't ever agree, it seems. I try, but
it don't seem to do any good. I have prayed these last few
days, I hope you don't ever feel sorry."

The new arrangement did not go smoothly, and by the
end of a year he and Ed had a single room by themselves.
The real-estate office had failed, and he had to strike out
again, with "the same old trepidation." He drove a laundry
truck, and then became a bill collector for a furniture company that sold on the installment plan. He was "a gabby
and sociable" collector, and was fascinated by these jobs
because they took him all over the city and brought him
into contact with all sorts of people; he even caught avid
glimpses into wealthy homes. But he was to be fired for the
episode that so shocked some reviewers of his autobiography. He was longing for a stylish overcoat with a satin
lining, and withheld twenty-five dollars from his accounts
to buy one. He was shortly found out, but was so terrified

and filled with shame that his employer simply let him go without pressing any charges. But from this searing event Dreiser dated the end of his youth.

He reflected on his type of mind as by then revealed. He was always more interested in seeing than in reading, in the spectacle of the ever-changing city. But what did he take in from what he saw? He recalled how at sixteen he had stared at a streetcar strike without any notion of what it meant, of the economic conditions that had caused it. Yet he had apparently absorbed "its surface forms" so thoroughly that he had stored them up for future use when he would have come also to understand "its internal nature."

He thought of himself as unusually unformed at nineteen and twenty. But he had grasped one central strand of his later philosophy in his eager acceptance of change. This was his response to the time-spirit of a region where everything old was held to be outmoded, everything new to be good. Dreiser would begin a philosophical essay on this theme: "If I were to preach any doctrine to the world, it would be love of change, or at least lack of fear of it." He would continue: "By change have come all the charms . . . of which our consciousness is aware. . . . Not that anything so much more perfect is in store . . . but that a different thing is at hand, always, outside your door, around the corner, beyond the limits of the vision of even the philosopher and thinker."

In his Chicago youth he had formulated nothing so extensive. To that period in particular he applied one of his most frequently quoted sentences of self-description: "Chronically nebulous, doubting, uncertain, I stared and stared at everything, only wondering, not solving." But the city began to call out from him vaguely shaped "word-pictures or rhapsodies" to its living splendor. Like Whitman discovering his New York, Dreiser walked the streets orating to himself. He sent in a heap of fevered manuscripts to Eugene Field's column, but these sketches were too poor even to be acknowledged.

He had not really conceived of himself as a writer, but he began to think now that he ought to try to get onto a newspaper. Yet how could he rise to such an exciting position, he "a mere collector by trade"? He hung around the offices, and after several rejections he was given a temporary assignment when new men were needed at the time of the Democratic national convention in 1892. Altgeld was to be elected governor that fall, but Dreiser seems to have paid little attention to this fact or to the rapidly rising Populist party, of which the young Chicago lawyer Clarence Darrow was keenly observant. "The things called property interests," Dreiser was to say, "were as yet beyond me. My mind was too much concerned with the poetry of life to busy itself with such minor things as politics."

But he now found he had a flair for the "feature" story of human interest, in the then current vogue of distant imitation of Dickens, and was taken on regularly by the *Globe*, a by no means distinguished paper. His first success was with a piece for its Sunday magazine on Chicago's worst slum, between Halstead Street and the river, to gather material for which he wandered around its clattering boardwalks and murky alleys between one and four in its strident mornings. "Why, I could write reams upon any topic when at last I discovered that I could write at all." The copious, often turgid, flow of words, responding to the rhythms of his feelings and struggling to reproduce them, set up what were to remain the lifelong habits of his writing.

His real education in understanding the kind of America to which he belonged took place in the newspaper world, and much of it was the product of several striking personalities upon his still impressionable mind. He never forgot the cynical well-read copy editor John Maxwell who helped and encouraged him with his writing while saying at the same time: "Life is a god-damned stinking, treacherous game, and nine hundred and ninety-nine men out of every thousand are bastards." John T. McEnnis, the heavy-drinking managing editor, took a fancy to him, also believed that he was going to be able to write, and advised him to give himself a general education by going to lectures and studying more. He wanted him to broaden out by working on a great paper, and after a few months insisted that he go to St. Louis with a letter of introduction to Joseph B. McCullagh, the "Little Mac" of Field's verse, one of the best-known journalists of the day.

Again, though Dreiser did not know it, this was to be a farewell. He only knew that it meant breaking off his first prolonged love affair, with a working girl he had met through one of his sisters. His desperate shyness and dread had at last worn off, and he could relax into her simple affection. "Was I in love with her? No, as I understand myself now. I doubt that I have ever been in love with anyone or anything save life as a whole."

Leaving his family now meant merely letting fall ties that had already been broken. Although Dreiser is often spoken of as a Chicago writer, he was never again to make his home in Chicago. He had watched from a distance George Ade and Finley Peter Dunne, who, four or five years older than himself, were already launched on their careers as brilliant reporters. He was to see a little of Hamlin Garland and to meet Henry B. Fuller, though not until twenty years later, when he had finished *The Financier* and come back to Chicago for a couple of months to gather material for *The Titan*. At that time he was also to meet Masters, and to begin his long if intermittent intimacy with him. At that time, too, Floyd Dell, then at the center of the new Chicago group, was to say: "The poetry of Chicago has been adequately rendered so far, by only one writer, and in only one book —*Sister Carrie*."

Newspaper Days

DREISER preserved a partly amused, partly indulgent portrait of himself as a young man of the nineties: "A dreamy cub of twenty-one, long, spindling, a pair of gold-framed spectacles on his nose, his hair combed *à la pompadour*, a new spring suit consisting of light check trousers and bright blue coat and vest, a brown fedora hat, new yellow shoes . . . I had already attained my full height, six feet one-and-one-half inches, and weighed only one hundred and thirty-seven pounds, so you can imagine my figure. Aside from one eye (the right) which was turned slightly outward from the line of vision, and a set of upper teeth which because of their exceptional size were crowded and so stood out too much, I had no particular blemish except a general homeliness of feature. It was a source of worry to me all the time, because I imagined that it kept me from being interesting to women; which, apparently, was not true—not to all women at least. Spiritually I was what might be called a poetic melancholiac, crossed with a vivid materialistic lust of life."

He appeared very uncertain, yet whenever his own deepest interests stirred him he could be adamant. He said that "love of beauty as such—feminine beauty, first and fore-most, of course—was the dominating characteristic of all my moods." Yet he also remembered: "My eyes were con-stantly fixed on people in positions far above my own. Those who interested me most were bankers, millionaires, artists, executives, leaders, the real rulers of the world." He wanted to get up—"oh, how eagerly." He went around say-ing to himself: "No common man am I."

He was often swayed by a dangerous ambivalence. When his thoughts were turned upon his own flimsy chances in the "gross favoritism" of existence, he sank into suicidal depressions. But when his attention was caught out of himself once more, he felt that he was "swimming in a delicious sea of life." In retrospect he could reflect: "I was always lucky—I always got the breaks." But at the time his strongest resource in exorcising the temptation of self-pity was what would also yield the deepest quality in his fiction: "an intense sympathy for the woes of others, life in all its helpless degradation and poverty, the unsatisfied dreams of people, their sweaty labors, the things they were compelled to endure—nameless impositions, curses, brutal-ities—the things they would never have, their hungers, thirsts, half-formed dreams of pleasure, their gibbering in-sanities and beaten resignations at the end."

Among the pieces that he wrote for the keen-minded rugged McCullagh on the St. Louis *Globe-Democrat* was a series of real and imaginary interviews, many of the latter springing from what Dreiser termed his "asinine ebulli-ence." But besides conjuring up characters with interesting philosophies, he also sought out a number of famous per-sonalities as they passed through the city. He had the same "favorite question" for all of them: "What did they think about life?" When applied successively to the explorer Stanley, the scientist Nikola Tesla, John L. Sullivan, and Annie Besant, this yielded fascinating answers.

He continued to find, as he had in Chicago, that he could derive "color" from even the most sordid aspects of the city. But he also perceived that hard ferretlike qualities were needed for a successful reporter. As so often in his life he felt himself divided: sometimes shamefaced and almost sick at the thought that he was spying on others' misfortunes, at other times swept by the love of the chase and exulting in his occasional triumphant scooping of a fellow reporter. He experienced this division most acutely when he happened to witness the explosion of an oil-tank car after a train wreck. Many people died before his eyes, but he was thinking only of how he would describe this. Yet when he went on to the morgue, he was suddenly swept with a sense of "the nothingness of man." And again the next morning he thrilled with vanity over the thought that everyone must be reading his account. McCullagh gave him a raise.

"Crazy for advancement," he angled for the post of theatrical reviewer. He did not realize that he was "neither old nor cold nor experienced enough to do justice to the art of anyone." This did not actually make much difference, since all that was required was to write a little two-stick notice, mainly favorable, of each new show. But he was presently to find himself ridiculed for praising a Negro singer for the sublety of her gifts. Negroes were not so described in St. Louis. And then he lost his job through a ludicrous miscalculation. He was sent out of town on an unexpected assignment one evening when three shows were scheduled to open; and so he followed the regular practice and wrote up routine accounts of their reception. These appeared, but unfortunately the theater companies had not, there having been washouts on the road.

Dreiser quit without even waiting to be summoned by McCullagh, but presently managed to be taken on by the rival *Republic*. Here the city editor kept telling him to remember Balzac and Zola, writers of whom Dreiser had barely heard. But their talents were hardly required when he was assigned to write a series of articles building up interest in a baseball game between the fat men and the thin men. He faced this with misgivings, he who had never written "anything funny" in his life. The result was lumberingly facetious, but it proved to be a success and led to another feature assignment. This was to accompany the winners of a statewide popularity contest for schoolteachers to the Chicago World's Fair, and to report their trip. Here was the kind of episode in Dreiser's life over which Mencken would chortle most profanely. He himself admitted that he "felt like a boob" in the flustering midst of such a chattering and giggling bevy. But he was put at his ease by the quiet natural manner of Sara White, a little red-haired teacher from a country town. His growing feeling for her was interwoven with his excitement over the Fair. Yet he found himself flirting also with another more sexually experienced girl. Aware that his feelings were "light and variable," he was puzzled, and not for the last time, by the fact that he was drawn to two girls at once. Yet Sallie White's gentle reserve gave him a new sense "of peace and support."

But the biggest influences upon him during his St. Louis days were two of his newspaper associates, Peter B. McCord, the illustrator, and Robert Hazard, a fellow reporter. Both were to die early, by pneumonia and suicide. Dreiser sketched McCord in *Twelve Men*, remarking that his own "swiftest developments mentally" had been "through men, not women. . . . Nearly every turning point in my career has been signalised by my meeting some man of great force, to whom I owe some of the most ecstatic intellectual hours of my life." Through McCord in particular he believed that he had gained some of his "sanest conceptions." The illustrator was forever noting "crass chance" and "fierce brutalities" in the struggle for existence, and yet accepted nature in its entirety with a delight that was tonic to Dreiser's still frequently fear-ridden mind. McCord encouraged him to relax by saying: "You don't know how to make anything out of the little things of life." He also suggested wider intellectual horizons through his own absorbed reading of archeology and ethnology, of Darwin and Taine. "And the mere word *art*," as Dreiser noted simply, "although I had no real understanding of it, was fascinating to me."

But the reading that made the greatest impression on him just then was the manuscript of a novel by Hazard and another young reporter. This was Dreiser's first introduction, at second hand, to the French authors whose names the city editor dinned into his ears. The scene was laid in Paris—which neither of its authors had visited—and its actress heroine Theo was not unrelated to Nana, though Dreiser could not recognize this. What impressed him most was the way Hazard took it for granted that a book like this could not be printed in America. "That struck me as odd at the time—the fact that if one wrote a fine thing, nevertheless because of an American standard I had not even thought of before, one might not get it published. How queer, I thought. Yet these two incipient artists had already encountered it. They had been overawed to the extent of thinking it necessary to write of French, not American life in terms of fact. Such things as they felt called upon to relate occurred only in France, never here—or at least such things, if done here, were never spoken of." Yet every day as a reporter Dreiser was encountering scenes that made such "moral hypocrisy" no better than "the trashiest lie."

Stimulated by the talk of these friends and brooding over the tangled unclearness of his existence, Dreiser "sat looking into the face of the tangle as one might into the gathering front of a storm. Words moved in my brain, then bubbled, then marshalled themselves into curious lines and rhythms. I put my pencil to paper, and wrote line after line. Presently I saw that I was writing a poem but that it was rough and needed modifying and polishing. I was in a great fever to change it and did so, but more eager to go on with my idea." Here is further reinforcement of what we noted about his first "rhapsodies" in Chicago, a practice that would remain with him. His fiction would rise from deep rhythms of feeling, but unfortunately it would be characteristic of his writing habits to the end of his life that he would always be hurrying beyond the words to develop the idea that was mastering him.

When Hazard learned that Dreiser was trying to write a poem, he suggested that he turn to "a book or a play"—a book, in the newspaper world, meaning a novel, of course. Dreiser was thrilled "at being considered a writer," but he was still far from being a judge of his own talents. For what he attempted was the text for a comic opera dealing with a cranky Indiana farmer who was suddenly transported back into Aztec times. The scenes sought their humor in that incongruity, but Dreiser found no one even to try the music.

He did not say whether he discussed it with Paul, who came to St. Louis with a melodrama in which he sang his newest song, about the Bowery. But Paul seems to have been impressed by his young brother's development, and talked to him about coming to New York. By now he was seriously courting Sallie White, attracted by everything about her that was least like his own surroundings: by her demureness and innocent sweetness, by the idyllic serenity which he connected with her father's farm. He knew that he must have made a "gawking and mooning" lover, and one of Sallie's friends remembered him as looking "like a big silly. He wore bicycle pants and a silly little cap and fancy stockings on his skinny legs"—though he brought no bicycle. Some of Dreiser's friends warned him against marrying her on the ground that Sallie, being a few years older than himself, would prove too settled into conventional ways to be responsive to his broader and less stable nature. But by the time he had decided to strike out for the East, in the spring of 1894, they were already engaged. Yet, sensing possible change in himself, he felt "sorry for her—for life—even then."

What caused him to give up his job in St. Louis was the half-formed plan, advanced by a reporter from Ohio, that they should get control of an Ohio country newspaper. This possibility fizzled out quickly, but Dreiser kept on to Toledo and, on the off chance of finding an opening, presented himself to the city editor of the *Blade*. Arthur Henry turned out to be only a little older than Dreiser, and a curious sense of affinity sprang up between them almost at once. Dreiser was to speak of him with a greater intensity than of any of his previous friends. What resulted was "an enduring and yet stormy and disillusioning friendship. If he had been a girl I would have married him, of course. It would have been inevitable. . . . Our dreams were practically identical, though we approached them from different angles. He was the sentimentalist in thought, the realist in action; I was the realist in thought and the sentimentalist in action. . . . He had dreams of becoming a poet and novelist, I of becoming a playwright. Meanwhile we reveled in that wonderful possession, intellectual affection."

But beyond a four-day spot assignment to cover a streetcar strike there was no opening on the *Blade*, and Dreiser had to move on again. "I was an Ishmael, a wanderer," he said, instinctively applying to himself the name that many other American writers besides Melville have believed to symbolize their relation with the world. He was now very restless. He went on to Cleveland where the prospects were discouraging, and to Buffalo where he was convinced even before he asked that he would secure no employment.

In the spring of 1894 the whole country was filled with restlessness. A couple of weeks before Dreiser arrived in Pittsburgh in mid-April "Coxey's Army" had camped there on its way to Washington. Dreiser was beginning to have some comprehension of industrial struggle. Along the Buffalo waterfront he "could not help but see that in spite of our boasted democracy and equality of opportunity, there was as much misery and squalor and as little decent balancing of opportunity against energy as anywhere else in the world." In St. Louis he had covered a speech by Terence V. Powderly still "perfectly ignorant" as to the rights of capital and labor, and thinking of himself as somehow superior to workmen. He had not been sharp or practical enough to grasp the significance of the panic of 1893. At

Toledo he had found that his sympathies were all with the strikers, but he seems not to have paid much attention to the great Pullman strike in Chicago this summer, or to the fact that this brought to national prominence a fellow-native of Terre Haute, Eugene Debs, who had been born there sixteen years before Dreiser.

In Pittsburgh he was taken on as a reporter by the *Dispatch*, and his education in the nature of society was continued by long talks with Martyn, its labor reporter. Dreiser could sense a kind of "sullen despair" as the aftermath of the Homestead defeat of two years before. He was quickly assured that "the steel people have this town sewed up tight," that "all you can do is to write what the people at the top want you to write, and that's very little." Hard-bitten by what he had seen, Martyn had grown to believe that "the cause of the workers everywhere in America was hopeless. They hadn't the subtlety and the force of the innate cruelty of those who ruled them." Dreiser was depressed by this, and by "the vast gap" he could see for himself here between rich and poor. But he was also dazzled by the magnificent mansions at Schenley Park.

He had to interview Thomas B. Reed, about to be re-elected Speaker of the House of Representatives, who was in town to consult with a friendly magnate and who told him that Coxey's Army constituted "a vast national menace." Dreiser could not believe this; in his eyes the "army" was only "a band of poor mistaken theorists" who imagined that they could compel "a trust-dictated American Senate" to take cognizance of their woes. In this detachment he was unlike Jack London, five years his junior, who had started east from San Francisco with a branch of the "army," had deserted at Hannibal, Missouri, when food ran out, and roamed the country as a tramp. He rode the rails to New York this midsummer, was picked up a few days later in Niagara Falls as a vagrant, and was sent to jail for a month along with fifteen other men by a judge who did not even bother to go through the form of asking them "Guilty, or not guilty?" This was the beginning of London's experience with class justice, and it started him on the way to becoming a socialist.

Dreiser was assigned mainly to "human interest" stories this summer, and produced pieces light in subject and tone. But he felt himself increasingly preoccupied with "the larger and more tragic phases of life," with the "huge and massive conditions" underlying them. When he took a trip out to see his fiancée on her Missouri farm, he realized more forcibly than ever before the distance the American present had gone from the American past, the distance, too, between the ideal and the actual: "We Americans have home traditions or ideals, created as much by song and romance as anything else: *My Old Kentucky Home, Suwanee River.* Despite any willing on my part, this home seemed to fulfill the spirit of those songs. . . . The shade of the great trees moved across the lawn in stately and lengthening curves. . . . Hammocks of barrel-staves, and others of better texture, were strung beneath the trees. In a nearby barn of quaint design were several good horses, and there were cows in the field adjoining. Ducks and geese solemnly paddled to and fro between the house and the stream. The air was redolent of corn, wheat, clover, timothy, flowers.

"To me it seemed that all the spirit of rural America, its idealism, its dreams, the passion of a Brown, the courage and patience and sadness of a Lincoln, the dreams and courage of a Lee or a Jackson, were all here. The very soil smacked of American idealism and faith, a fixedness in sentimental and purely imaginative American tradition, in which I, alas! could not share. I was enraptured. Out of its charms and sentiments I might have composed an elegy or an epic, but I could not believe that it was more than a frail flower of romance. I had seen Pittsburgh. I had seen Lithuanians and Hungarians in their 'courts' and hovels. I had seen the girls of that city walking the streets at night. The profound faith in God, in goodness, in virtue and duty that I saw here in no wise squared with the craft, the cruelty, the brutality and the envy that I saw everywhere else."

The mood in which he wrote this passage was intermingled with his feeling that, unknown to him at the time, this summer had also witnessed the beginning of the end of his love for Sallie. He could condense the reason into a sentence: "Glorious fruit that hangs upon the vine too long, and then decays." Together constantly on the farm, he was attracted by her more and more physically: "I wanted to take her then and not wait, but the prejudices of a most careful rearing frightened and deterred her. And yet I shall always feel that the impulse was better than the forces which confronted and subsequently defeated it. . . . Nature's way is correct, her impulses sound." But they could not afford to get married—at any rate would not till more than four years later. By then, "the first flare of love had thinned down to the pale flame of duty. . . . The first law of convention had been obeyed, whereas the governing forces of temperament had been overridden—and with what results eventually you may well suspect."

The floundering confusions of Dreiser's mind this summer were dramatized, if not resolved, by his first really mature reading—of the two major authors who were to have the profoundest effect upon him. One afternoon he picked up *The Wild Ass's Skin* in the Carnegie Library, and had the sensation of viewing "a prospect so wide that it left me breathless—all Paris, all France." He devoured in rapid succession four more of Balzac's novels, and was fascinated to discover that "the types he handled with most enthusiasm and skill—the brooding, seeking, ambitious beginner[s] in life's social, political, artistic and commercial affairs (Rastignac, Raphael, de Rubempré, Bianchon)—were . . . so much like myself."

The kinship was closest in *The Great Man of the Provinces in Paris*. In its very opening chapter Lucien de Rubempré is made aware of the enormous importance of the right clothes, and they remain one of Balzac's most recurrent symbols for luxury. A few pages later the novelist is reflecting that "the anguish of the poor and the unfortunate, from whatever cause it comes, is not less deserving of attention than the crises which revolutionize the lives of the powerful and the privileged of the earth." Although Lucien was hardly poor in the sense that Dreiser was, he was continually conscious of the gulf that separated him from the rich. He was the outsider, with an intense desire to move *up* and *in*. The high society to which Lucien aspired was as far from Dreiser's experience as was *The Arabian Nights*, but Dreiser already knew much of the cynical realm of journalism in which Lucien tried to thrive. In Balzac's sweeping panorama of Paris, "the capital of chance," of the materialism of society and the animality of man, of a thoroughly amoral world in which greed and self-interest are "squatting in every corner" and where money-values alone prevail, Dreiser felt that he was not far from Pittsburgh. "I was in a workaday, begrimed, and yet vivid Paris. Taillefer, Nucingen, Valentin were no different from some of the immense money magnates here, in their ease, luxury, power, at least the possibilities which they possessed."

At this moment Dreiser aspired not to be Balzac, but to be one of Balzac's heroes. Their images of glamour reinforced the vague longings he had had, as he walked along Euclid Avenue in Cleveland and stared at the new mansions of Rockefeller and Flagler. He perceived in himself no skills for making money; yet, yearning none the less hungrily for what money would buy, he indulged in the crudest chromo dream of somehow enthralling an heiress and moving into her realm of splendor and ease.

A few months later he read Spencer's *First Principles* and became one of the thousands of Americans for whom this constituted a catalyzing event. Spencer's thought operated in several different spheres, especially after he became in this country the philosopher of those who ordinarily did not read philosophy. In his broadest sweep he helped release many readers from the bonds of orthodox dogma by acquainting them for the first time with purely naturalistic arguments. Those who were seeking to replace the dogma they had already left behind them with something positive and purposive, Spencer's matter-of-fact synthesis served as it did Jack London's autobiographical hero, Martin Eden: "organizing all knowledge for him, reducing everything to unity, elaborating ultimate realities, and presenting to his startled gaze a universe so concrete of realization that it was like the model of a ship such as sailors make and put into glass bottles." American optimistic faith in the doctrine of progress found support in Spencer's evolutionary teaching, whereas our conservative politicians could cite his belief in *laissez faire* against all reformers. When the younger Oliver

Wendell Holmes, already a notable lawyer, remarked in this same year that no other contemporary writer save Darwin had so affected our way of thinking, he meant something not quite the same as what Andrew Carnegie meant by saying that Spencer was "the man to whom I owe most." It was at this point that dominant American behavior became a vast caricature of his doctrines. Taking Spencer's phrase "the Survival of the Fittest" at its face value, our captains of industry and their apologists proved with strenuous satisfaction that inequality was the natural law of the struggle for existence, and that their own careers were inevitable.

Dreiser, who also read Huxley's *Science and Christian Tradition*, believed that this naturalistic strain of thought released him from the last vestiges of Catholicism which he had found so oppressive. In *First Principles* he gave closest attention to Spencer's detailed formulation and illustration of the law of evolution, to the argument that the Persistence of Force is the ultimate basis of knowledge. He appears to have paid less heed at this time to Spencer's doctrine of the Unknowable, the means by which the philosopher separated the realms of science and religion, not by denying the absolute but by relegating it to the realm of nescience and mystery. Not until his later years would Dreiser move beyond the confines of Spencer's mechanism through pondering more and more this mysterious Unknowable.

In an editorial written a couple of years after this first reading, he would recommend Spencer on the ground that he could marshal "the whole universe in review before you . . . showing you how certain beautiful laws exist, and how, by these laws, all animate and inanimate things have developed and arranged themselves." But this serene acceptance does not really represent Spencer's first impact upon him. It blew him "intellectually to bits." Dreiser's life so far had left him with very little of our middle-class optimism, and though he would be compelled to acknowledge "the survival of the fittest" as an accurate description of the inequalities that he found more and more characteristic of our economy, he could take no satisfaction in this as one of the submerged unfit. Pondering Spencer's cool proposition that "life in its simplest form is the correspondence of certain inner physico-chemical actions with certain outer physico-chemical actions," his own emotion warped it into something far less objective: "Up to this time there had been in me a blazing and unchecked desire to get on and the feeling that in doing so we did get somewhere; now in its place was the definite conviction that spiritually one got nowhere . . . that one lived and had his being because one had to, and that it was of no importance. Of one's ideals, struggles, deprivations, sorrows and joys, it could only be said that they were chemic compulsions, something which for some inexplicable but unimportant reason responded to and resulted from the hope of pleasure and the fear of pain. Man was a mechanism, undevised and uncreated, and a badly and carelessly driven one at that."

In the light of such a passage it seems futile to regret that at this crucial stage in his development Dreiser did not come upon a more adequate philosophy than Spencer's mechanism. Dreiser possessed none of the cultural background which enabled William James to describe Spencer's mind as "so fatally lacking in geniality, humor, picturesqueness and poetry; and so explicit, so mechanical, so flat in the panorama which it gives to life." And Dreiser's lack of equipment would probably have prevented him from grasping any less barely schematized or more resilient system. Once he had adjusted himself to his initial shock he found in Spencer's principles at least a guide through the labyrinthine jungle with which he was surrounded. Yet the road which Spencer opened before him was not one he could contemplate without great pain:

"All I could think of was that since nature would not or could not do anything for man, he must, if he could, do something for himself; and of this I saw no prospect, he being a product of these self-same accidental, indifferent and bitterly cruel forces. And so I went on from day to day, reading, thinking, doing fairly acceptable work, but always withdrawing more and more into myself. As I saw it then, the world could not understand me, nor I it, nor men each other very well. Then a little later I turned and said that since the whole thing was hopeless I might as well forget it and join the narrow heartless indifferent scramble, but I could not do that either, lacking the temperament and the skill. All I could do was think, and since no paper such as I knew was interested in any of the things about which I was thinking, I was hopeless indeed. Finally, in late November, having two hundred and forty dollars saved, I decided to leave this dismal scene and seek the charm of the great city beyond, hoping that there I might succeed at something, be eased and rested by some important work of some kind."

A Young Man
of the Provinces in New York

PAUL had said: "You'll be like everybody else—there'll be just one place—New York." But Dreiser was "very much afraid" of the city at first, though it was to become his chief home for over forty years. At his arrival, in addition to Paul, two of his sisters were also established there, one of them married, the other living with the man with whom she had eloped from Chicago. Somewhat later Ed would come there as an actor.

The city to which Paul introduced him was not the one out of which Edith Wharton was to make her stories, contrasting the values of the older aristocracy with those of the new commercialism. Nor was it the city of political corruption which Lincoln Steffens was just beginning to investigate so shrewdly. Nor was it the one of music and the arts which James G. Huneker was hoping might soon begin to compare in quality with Europe. It was Paul's city of actors and sports, the Broadway of the Martinique and the Metropole, of Muldoon the famous wrestler and Tod Sloan the jockey, of Tony Pastor's and Niblo's and Weber & Fields.

Since their mother's death Dreiser found much to remind him of her in Paul's voice and manner—"the same wonder, the same wistfulness and sweetness, the same bubbling charity and tenderness of heart." Paul had no interest in books or ideas, and would not have the least understanding of his brother's aims as a writer, but he was always full of encouragement for him. At the top of his popularity now as a song writer, he had a Falstaffian figure and appetite for pleasure. He was gross and sensual, with a love for many women, and an addiction to humor that was often horseplay and that sometimes broke into tearful sentiment. Dreiser saw himself in contrast as still "a thin, spindling, dyspeptic, and disgruntled youth." But Paul would clap him on the back, and escort him gaily up Broadway, from one brightly lighted spot to another.

The city he discovered for himself was "so huge and powerful and terrible" that it added further to his feeling of uselessness. Yet it fascinated him, too, it was so varied and alluring, if, above all, so hard. The gulf between rich and poor was wider and deeper even than it had been in Pittsburgh, and seemed to produce an "air of ruthlessness and indifference and disillusion." Keenly aware of these things, as well as of the brutality that underlay the city's social structure, Henry George would run again for mayor in the next campaign, though it would exhaust him to the point of death.

Casting about for a foothold, Dreiser quickly learned that he was no longer regarded as a star reporter. In Cleveland the Sunday editor of the *Plain Dealer* had told him that he "rhapsodized" too much, but here he had a hard time even to get beyond the insolent office boys. He finally secured a routine police-court assignment on the *World*.

Pulitzer had been building up this paper for a decade, but Dreiser was soon dismayed at the contrast between "the professed ideals and preachments of such a constantly moralizing journal" and "the heartless and savage aspect of its internal economy." Pulitzer's aggressive, restless ambition had produced an office where, whatever it may have been for successful figures like David Graham Phillips, all the underlings appeared to Dreiser to feel a "sword of disaster" suspended over them, the sword of bitter reprimand or contempt or dismissal. In consequence they had "a kind of nervous, resentful terror in their eyes as have animals when they are tortured. . . . Every man was for himself."

He had already begun to reflect that reporting was at best "a boy's game," suited only to the push of brazen energies. But now his misgivings deepened. As he pondered all he had learned "about the subservience of newspapers to financial interests, their rat-like fear of religionists and moralists, their shameful betrayal of the ordinary man at every point at which he could possibly be betrayed, yet still having the power, by weight of lies and pretence and make-believe, to stir him up to his detriment and destruction," Dreiser was "frightened by this very power, which in subsequent years I have come to look upon as the most deadly and forceful of all in nature: the power to masquerade and betray."

But what else could he do? He had no other trade or profession. He had some vague thoughts of trying to write short stories, but as he examined the current *Century* or *Harper's* for clues as to what might be accepted, he was confounded by the discrepancy between his own observations and "those displayed here, the beauty and peace and charm to be found in everything, the almost complete absence of any reference to the coarse and the vulgar and the cruel and the terrible." On the other hand, it was no comfort to turn to Vance Thompson's sophisticated *M'lle New York* and to see listed among the enemies of any flowering of American culture "dull melancholiacs in the gray provinces, lean pessimists of Kansas and the West."

He was haunted by the thought that he might have to give up and leave. And in spite of all the fierceness of the struggle in New York, he was held by "the magnetism of large bodies over small ones." Yet one wintry day, when he sat down dejected among the unemployed and the tramps on a bench in City Hall Park, he was overwhelmed by the contrast between their world and the world of success pursued in the tall offices soaring above them. In such contrasts, if one possessed the steadiness to fathom them, lay essential American drama. Dreiser was to say that at this moment "the idea of Hurstwood was born."

He was near the edge of real poverty himself during the summer of 1895, after quitting the *World* in discouragement over getting nothing but marginal assignments. Paul was away with a show, and Dreiser, looking in vain for any other work, was living at a cheap hotel little better than a flop-house. He was picked up and taken in for the night by an Italian girl, who then unexpectedly offered him a free room over her father's restaurant. But, thinking of his fiancée, he did not go back. What he remembered longest from this period was endless walks through the Bowery: "I was never able to get the spectacle out of my mind. It caused me to fear for myself—that in due course I might possibly land here—this region of forgotten men."

In the fall there was an opening for him as editor of a magazine that Paul's music publishers were starting. Dreiser himself suggested the title, *Ev'ry Month*, and was in full charge of its contents, which consisted mainly of the new songs. But he could also select stories, though he wrote none himself, and he furnished monthly editorials. These were toned to the magazine level, so that when he wrote about Spencer he only skimmed the surface of his thoughts. Most of his other pieces reflect the timely interests of the moment: atrocities in Armenia, graft in New York City, the possibilities of life on Mars. He came nearest to his own real knowledge when he discussed the immense wealth lavished on luxuries and the wretchedness of the sweatshops.

His first words to gain any wide currency were those he furnished for what was to prove Paul's greatest hit. One day when Paul was stuck for a subject, Dreiser suggested—without giving it much thought since he always felt himself a little "superior" to Paul's banal lyrics—that he might try a song about a state or a river, that people liked those. "Take Indiana—what's the matter with it—the Wabash River? It's as good as any other river, and you were 'raised' beside it." When Paul urged him to do the words himself, he balked, but then relaxing to the occasion, he jotted down, if both a little scornfully and shamefacedly, the first stanza and the chorus of "On the Banks of the Wabash, Far Away." But by the time Paul's tune was being whistled and sung all over the country, the brothers were going through a period of estrangement. Dreiser ultimately blamed himself entirely for this, "vain and yet more or less dependent snip that I was." He seems to have felt that Paul was patronizing him. He added, in a sentence which throws into a grim light the dour and suspicious strain from his father that he was to bring to many relationships: "I was very difficult to deal with."

His editorship took him a rung or two up the New York

ladder, and in a couple of years he could resign it to trust himself to free-lance writing for *Ainslee's,* the *Cosmopolitan,* and other magazines. Before the turn of the century he had produced nearly a hundred articles, interviews, and essays, though it comes as a surprise to learn that he gained a place in the first issue of *Who's Who in America,* in 1899. But after noting in its preface that it has included a large number of journalists, this volume lists him as "Journalist—author . . . contributes prose and verse to various periodicals. Author: Studies of Contemporary Celebrities; Poems."

His articles could hardly have been more miscellaneous, and serve as an index to what was needed to get on. They deal with "American Women Who Play the Harp," "Carrier Pigeons in War Time," "The Harlem Speedway," "An Invention That Will Make Electricity Cheap Enough for Economical Domestic Use," "The Chicago Packing Industry," "The Career of a Modern Portia, Mrs. Clara Shortridge Foltz," and so on. Several on literary men convey little more than the prevailing thinness of the atmosphere: "The Haunts of Bayard Taylor," "Edmund Clarence Stedman at Home," "Anthony Hope Tells a Secret." This last was part of a long series he did for *Success,* a magazine edited by Orison Swett Marden, which was wholly in the Horatio Alger strain. The only pieces that were to provide Dreiser with some material he could use for a different purpose later were his interviews with Chauncey Depew, Armour, Field, Edison, and Carnegie. Men like these set the tone for the world in which Frank Cowperwood found himself. But for this assignment Dreiser had to write of them almost purely in praise.

How perfunctory and blank were the results of the required formula can be read in "How William Dean Howells Climbed Fame's Ladder." After spending most of his space on the biographical record, Dreiser concluded with nothing more incisive than "His greatness is his goodness, his charm, his sincerity." We know from what Dreiser said later that Howells's work never gave him a sense of the America that he himself knew. And though Dreiser noted Howells's generosity in commending "quite unknown" authors, he was an enthusiastic champion of *Maggie: A Girl of the Streets* and *McTeague*, but not of *Sister Carrie*.

About the only interview that suggests a fertile interplay is the one with the young photographer Alfred Stieglitz, whose early experimental work, as Dreiser recognized, was still "greater than his reputation." In Stieglitz's street scenes, both uptown and downtown, Dreiser saw the authentic New York, and was equally impressed by the photographer's penetrating vision and by the "endless patience" with which he could wait three hours in the rain for the right moment. Pre-eminent among Dreiser's own qualities is what Dorothy Dudley called his "marvellous eye," which often went far to offset his inaccurate ear and fumbling sense of touch. It was the kind of eye that, without benefit of notebook, would tenaciously store up for many years the details for his autobiographies, to the point of this unnecessary but telling glimpse of Boss Croker at that Chicago convention which Dreiser covered as his first assignment: "the patent leather button shoes with gray suede tops, the heavy gold ring on one finger, and the heavy watch-chain across the chest."

Despite the listing in *Who's Who*, Dreiser never reprinted any of his interviews, and they were collected only in some compendiums by Marden, *Little Visits with Great*

Americans and *How They Succeeded*, without Dreiser's name. He apparently did have some hope of issuing a book of the poems which had constituted his first creative work. Several of these were scattered through the periodicals for which he was writing his articles, particularly in *Demorest's Family Magazine*. They bear such titles as "Night Song," "Bondage," "Resignation," "With Whom Is Shadow of Turning," "Through All Adversity." Their prevailing strains are grave and yearning, but their phrasing is almost entirely stock. They are really no more distinguished than the stanza and chorus for Paul, of which Dreiser thought so little. Like Whitman, who also began as a journalist, Dreiser turned for his first personal expression to the form which gentility rated high, the lyric of conventional mold. He could do nothing at all with it, and when he finally did publish a volume of poems, in the nineteen-twenties, he had turned entirely to free verse.

The only pieces of writing that he preserved from this period were two or three sketches that he included long afterwards in *The Color of a Great City*. These sketches, picking out striking details from Broadway or the waterfront, are still in the genre of the human-interest story with which he had started in Chicago half a dozen years before. But now he made a deliberate and very simplified analogy with Spencer's conception that all of existence is an equilibrium between rival forces. His version of this proposition was that "without contrast there is no life," and he applied it by saying that men lashed by a storm "are a bit of color in the city's life, whatever their sufferings." The detachment he gained through this attitude no doubt helped him control his material, but at this point it also deprived him of his greatest asset, his involved knowledge of such material.

Through regarding all of life as an external spectacle, his sketches had no more depth than a reporter's "copy."

By the time he was twenty-seven nothing that Dreiser had done gave promise of his being a writer of any note at all. But he had bucked the tide of the city to the extent of saving enough money to marry Sallie White in the Christmas season of 1898. The next summer he and his wife went to visit the Arthur Henrys in Maumee, Ohio. There Dreiser, very much dissatisfied with what he had been doing, listened at last to Henry's urging that he should try short-stories. The first one that he wrote, "McEwen of the Shining Slave Makers" was of a wholly different quality from anything he had done so far, his real start in his own kind of work. It may possibly have owed its germ to Dreiser's memory of a passage near the end of *The Wild Ass's Skin*, where Valentin, desperate at the thought of his impending death, seeks distraction in observing nature, and Balzac reflects: "Who has not, at some time or other in his life, watched the comings and goings of an ant . . . ?"

In Dreiser's story, McEwen, a newspaper man, sits down on a park bench on a hot August day, idly kills an ant running on the walk at his feet, and then, as he gazes at others swarming in all directions, suddenly discovers himself in their world. It is strange and yet the same as the world he has known, marked by selfishness and violence. There is egregious hoarding of food: "the indifference and sufficiency were at once surprising and yet familiar." He watches another ant stiffening into death. "Had he not, in times past, reported the deaths of hundreds?" A war breaks out between the reds and the blacks, in which he gains companionship, but eventually also his own destruction.

At that moment McEwen opened his eyes and saw the

ground at his feet strewn with dead ants: "What was this—
a revelation of the spirit and significance of a lesser life or
of his own—or what? . . . What worlds within worlds, all
apparently full of necessity, contention, binding emotions
and unities—all with sorrow, their sorrow . . . which had
been there, and was here in this strong bright city day, had
been there and would be here until this odd, strange thing
called *life* had ended."

Here is the earliest sample of the style that Dreiser would
be known by, the groping after words corresponding to the
groping of the thought, but with both words and thought
borne along on the diapason of a deep emotion. Here he has
found the right kind of detachment, not by reducing all of
life to a mere show, but by heightening its stature through
a somewhat clumsy but basically Swiftian satire. He may
have fallen into this instinctively rather than have planned
it out. But by the solid strength of what he had to say he
had broken away from all the current formulas for magazine fiction, as though a waking Gulliver were snapping
their flimsy strings.

To his surprise this story was accepted by *Ainslee's* for
seventy-five dollars, and thus encouraged he followed it up
with "When the Old Century Was New," "Old Rogaum
and His Theresa," and "Nigger Jeff"—all of which would
be printed in the next year or two. In the first of these he
showed, as though giving an object lesson to himself, how
completely he would fail if he tried to do the expected
thing. According to the vogue of historical romance, he
sketched a day in New York in 1801, with glimpses even of
Mr. Adams and Mr. Jefferson, but with nothing to distinguish it from other paper-thin period pieces.

In dealing with the tension between old Rogaum, a German butcher in Bleecker Street, and his seventeen-year-old daughter who has begun to loiter outdoors on summer evenings, Dreiser was again to gain the kind of simple largeness which came to him, not from trying to contrive a story, but from writing out of what he knew by heart. This could be his own family as the father, furious at the heedless girl, locks her out one night and then is filled with panic, so that when he finally gets her back unharmed he is too relieved to give her the threatened beating. But as Dreiser built up slowly to his single climax, he also produced a New York street scene of the patient fullness for which he so admired Stieglitz, stressing the kind of homely detail that George Luks aand John Sloan were beginning to stress, and that would win for them the scornful name of "the ash-can school."

"Nigger Jeff" is a passage in the education of a young reporter. He is sent out to cover a case in which a Negro has assaulted a white girl, in an unspecified countryside that would seem to be near St. Louis. He gradually realizes that he is to be a "hired spectator" of a lynching. The Negro had not previously done anything bad, except for drinking now and then, and it was because of drinking that he made his advances to the girl. He is caught by the sheriff because he stops to say good-bye to his mother.

When the gathering mob finally breaks in at night, the girl's father and brother strike the young reporter as "brutal," the injury done to the girl "not so vital as all this." Deeply shaken by the hanging, he suddenly sees life as "so sad, so strange, so mysterious, so inexplicable." Yet he continues to gather all the details for his story, even visiting the stricken mother of the Negro. The conclusion is part of Dreiser's development too: "The night, the tragedy, the grief, he saw it all. But also with the cruel instinct of the budding artist that he already was, he was beginning to meditate on the character of story it would make—the color, the pathos. The knowledge now that it was not always exact justice that was meted out to all and that it was not so much the business of the writer to indict as to interpret was borne in on him with distinctness by the cruel sorrow of the mother, whose blame, if any, was infinitesimal.

" 'I'll get it all in!' he exclaimed feelingly, if triumphantly at last. 'I'll get it all in!' "

Dreiser had now understood the kind of hardness that the artist must have, the hardness that will enable him to express what he has to say. But if his expression is to be of value, it must always remain rooted in such feelings as Dreiser brought to his experience from the days of his first reporting. "I was swelling with an excess of sympathy, wonder, respect, even awe." The four qualities he enumerates will run like a plain song through his best fiction.

A Picture of Conditions

THAT fall Arthur Henry, coming on to New York, challenged Dreiser to an agreement that they would both try their hands at novels. The circumstances of the writing and publishing of *Sister Carrie* and then of its virtual suppression constitute the best-known episode in Dreiser's story, the one that has been told most often to symbolize his career. He said that he sat down and wrote the words of his title at the top of a page without any clear idea of how he would proceed. "Yes, actually! My mind was a blank except for the name. I had no idea who or what she was to be. I have often thought there was something mystic about it, as if I were being used, like a medium." Yet he soon found that he had plenty to say, and wrote steadily for a month, the first hundred pages or so, up to where Drouet introduces Carrie to Hurstwood. Then, feeling that what he had done was a failure, he stopped, and turned to salable articles for a couple of months. At this point Henry put on his pressure, saying that unless Dreiser went on with his book, he could not go on with *A Princess of Arcady*. Dreiser therefore, laughing at himself as a fool, picked up his manuscript, but had to drop it "just before Hurstwood steals the money, because I couldn't think how to have him do it."

For a while in the early winter Henry was away, but when he came back he read what Dreiser had written and told him he must continue. Then, as Dreiser told Dorothy Dudley: "I managed to solve the problem, and for a while it went pretty good, until I came to the question of Hurst-wood's decline, which took me back to the *World* days. Then I had to stop again. Somehow I felt unworthy to write all that. It seemed too big, too baffling. . . . But after a month I managed to get the thread, and finished it up in May. Henry read it and said 'Don't change a word.' But I spent some weeks revising it; he helped me. In May or June 1900 I sent it to Harper's. I knew one of the editors. They refused it. Then I took it down to Doubleday's. In November it was out."

What did he have in mind when he put down those first two words? What conception of a novel was alive for him to draw upon? At the point in time at which Dreiser turned to fiction, one would have said that an American novelist might at last have felt that he had a tradition behind him that could help him find his way. Unlike Hawthorne or Melville, who had had the sensation of pioneering unaided through a wilderness, a man of Dreiser's day could have been aware of the thirty years in which Howells and James had been assimilating and acclimatizing the modes of realism. But Dreiser was either ignorant of this, or found it all beside his purposes.

The briefest way to describing either Dreiser or James is to say that he was everything the other was not. In later years Dreiser was to remark: "I would reject most of James as too narrowly and thinly class-conscious"—an indication that he could never have read James very carefully. When he started *Sister Carrie*—nearly fifteen years after *The Bostonians*, the last of James's novels until the posthumous *The Ivory Tower* to deal with America—Dreiser had certainly not read him at all. On the other hand, when James revisited America in 1904, he reflected that the titanic energies of New York demanded the crude powers of a Zola to encompass them. He had doubtless not even heard of *Sister Carrie*; indeed, many copies were then still stored in Doubleday's warehouse.

Howells and Dreiser, as we have seen, had hardly any more effectual communication. They were divided by the watershed, not only of two generations, but of two widely different views of American life and of the fiction needed to express it. Dreiser found Howells too tame—worse, "uninformed." He reported that Howells remarked to him one day in the street: "You know, I don't like *Sister Carrie*." And though Howells continued for a dozen years thereafter to comment on the work of younger writers, he seems not to have found anything to interest him in *Jennie Gerhardt* or *The Financier*. His own neat sense of style may well have been put off by Dreiser's clumsiness. But no wonder Dreiser would say: "Howells won't see American life as it is lived; he doesn't want to see it."

What could be made out of a growing American consciousness of a tradition in fiction may be instanced by the work of Edith Wharton. Nine years older than Dreiser, her problem was at the other extreme from his. She had to find her way out of a purely moneyed and social world, and James was of inestimable value in showing her that the materials of this world, held in ironic detachment, could also serve for fiction. But she had so much to unlearn that she did not hit her real stride until *The House of Mirth*, five years after *Sister Carrie*.

Two writers who had turned rather to Howells than to James were Hamlin Garland and Henry B. Fuller. Dreiser was to praise *Main-Travelled Roads* (1891) for the verity of its country types, and to state that *With the Procession* (1895) was "the first piece of American realism" he had encountered and that it gave him a glimpse of "the true Chicago American scene of the day," with its "post-Civil War commercial and social atmosphere." Fuller was really a fascinating cross between Howells and James. Strongly drawn to the psychological complexity and subtlety of *The Portrait of a Lady*, he nevertheless resolved that he should turn his back on James's Europe and work with the materials of his native city. This conflict—very real for his sensitive nature—produced a quiet intensity which made his contrast between the Chicago of the first settlers and that of the newer moneyed interests seem genuine to Dreiser in a way that Howells's honest but more external studies of Boston and New York never did.

The role of Dreiser's immediate contemporaries was to press beyond realism to naturalism. *The Red Badge of Courage* made a great stir the year that Dreiser first arrived in New York. But though he printed one of Crane's stories, "A Mystery of Heroism," in *Ev'ry Month*, he seems never to have had any feeling of close kinship with Crane's work. The case was altogether different with Frank Norris. Dreiser says that he picked up *McTeague* shortly after finishing *Sister Carrie*, and was thrilled by "the invaluable local color, the force and reality of it all. Here was a true book, as arresting and illuminating as any I had ever read, and about America!" When Dreiser submitted his manuscript to Doubleday, Norris turned out to be the reader, and declared that he had found "a masterpiece." "It was," he reported, "the best novel I had read . . . since I had been reading for the firm, and it pleased me as well as any novel I have read in *any* form, published or otherwise."

If Norris rather than Dreiser were under consideration here, this would be the point where we should have to examine the theories of naturalism. For Norris had read Zola while he was an art student in France, and in *McTeague* had set himself deliberately to emulate Zola's conception of man's animality; while in *The Octopus* he would try to evoke the huge forces in society which could sweep over the individual. To be sure, a detailed comparison with his master would reveal a lack of settled philosophical purpose and a boyish worship of force that he gave no signs of outgrowing. But Dreiser was to tell Mencken that he had "never read a line of Zola." He went on from Balzac to Hardy, whose sense of massive fate made a deep impression upon him. But the chief thing revealed through considering the aspects of tradition available for a writer of Dreiser's day is how little he was aware of them.

He is a primary example of the frequent American need to begin all over again from scratch. His case would seem to be different from that of Whitman, who found the gap so wide between what he had to say and any usual poetic form that he could not possibly bridge it. But in Whitman's day American poetry had hardly any tradition behind it, whereas fiction had been accruing a considerable background since Hawthorne had felt the thinness of his resources. Yet Dreiser was the representative of a far cruder America than Hawthorne's. He was only half-educated, and was scarcely a conscious artist at all when he set out to write *Sister Carrie.* In an authentic sense he was a primitive, not unlike the occasional American sign painter who has found that he possessed the dogged skills to create a portrait likeness, and then has bent all the force of a rugged character to realize this verity.

Opinions have been sharply divided as to Dreiser's skill in the most rudimentary element of his craft, the ability to tell a story. Some readers feel that he loses its movement in his crowded mass of details. But Ford Madox Ford held that "the difference between a supremely unreadable writer like Zola and a completely readable one like Dreiser is simply that if Zola had to write about a ride on a railway locomotive's tender or a night in a brothel, Zola had to get it all out of a book. Dreiser has only to call on his undimmed memories, and the episode will be there in all its freshness and vigor." Although the comparison seems to ignore the tremendous sweeping energy of (say) *Germinal,* and thus is unjust to Zola, Ford did hit at the center of what Dreiser has to offer. When he wrote *Sister Carrie,* he was hardly concerned with the intricacies of a plot as Hardy contrived one. So far as he was aware of a model at all, it was Balzac's direct way of presenting solid slabs of continuous experience. Looking back at the finished result, he said: "It is not intended as a piece of literary craftsmanship, but as a picture of conditions done as simply and effectively as the English language will permit." This dodges the question just as Whitman had done when he declared: "No one will get at my verses who insists upon viewing them as a literary performance." Their suspicion of the polite literature of their own times drove them both to this reckless extreme, and we may begin to understand Dreiser's feeling when we recall the reception of *Sister Carrie* by those who were looking for "literary" effects.

Why his "picture of conditions" then seemed revolutionary in America is perhaps the aspect of Dreiser that is hardest for us to grasp now. Yet, as Masters was to put it: "Forty years ago when you wrote *Sister Carrie*, there was one ideology by which to write the novel about a woman. It was to prove that as a matter of Christian sin, not even of cause and consequence . . . the woman was punished. You cleaned up the country and set the pace for the truth, and freed the young, and enlightened the old where they could be enlightened." Masters's rhetorical flourish sprang from his memory of how grimly oppressive the limitations of honest speech had been for a young man in 1900.

Carrie not only escaped punishment—Dreiser did not even regard her as sinful; and this was the crux of his defiance of late nineteenth-century conventionality. Only he hardly thought of it then as a defiance. He was simply writing what he knew. For doing no more—and no less—than this he would be hailed by Sherwood Anderson as the stalwart opener of doors for the next generation. Dorothy Dudley, who as a descendant of Fuller's inner Chicago and a graduate of Bryn Mawr, knew the convention from the inside, would strike as her leading theme that: "In the midst of a ruling tameness, or at least of a tameness dictated by those ruling here toward the last third of the last century, Dreiser was one of those born outside the convention, and living outside of it."

We have now moved so far from that convention that the contemporary effort to suppress *Sister Carrie* may strike us as only a curious freak—though we must not lose sight of the continuing effort today to suppress novels of more than

Dreiser's naturalistic frankness. For we have by now so long defied the genteel tradition that we now tend to idealize it, to feel a nostalgic longing for it as an escape from our world which seems to us so much more brutal than Dreiser's. But if we are to appreciate, not the final value of Dreiser to readers today, but the first great contribution that he brought to his contemporaries, we must remember that Santayana coined the phrase "the genteel tradition" to describe what he considered the most dangerous defect in American thought.

Observing our dominant New England culture, Santayana believed that its deep-rooted error was that it separated thought from experience. Among the legacies of a colonial culture is the habit of thinking of creative sources as somehow remote from itself, of escaping from the hardness and rawness of everyday surroundings into an idealized picture of civilized refinement, of believing that the essence of beauty must lie in what James Russell Lowell read about in Keats rather than in what Walt Whitman saw in the streets of Brooklyn. The inescapable result of this is to make art an adornment rather than an organic expression of life, to confuse it with politeness and delicacy. Even Howells, who set himself to record ordinary existence, could drift into saying: "Elsewhere we literary folk are apt to be such a common lot, with tendencies here and there to be a shabby lot . . . but at Boston we were of ascertained and noted origin, and a good part of us dropped from the skies. Instead of holding horses before the doors of theaters; or capping verses at the plow tail; or tramping over Europe with nothing but a flute in the pocket; or walking up to the metropolis with no luggage but the MS. of a tragedy; or sleeping in doorways or under the arches of bridges; or serving as apothecaries' prentices—we were good society from the beginning. I think this was none the worse for us, and it was vastly the better for good society."

With the last decades of the nineteenth century, as the new industrial cities filling up with new immigrants from central and southern Europe were less and less like London, the further mistake was made of thinking of literature as somehow dependent upon the better-born groups of richer standing. Even Edith Wharton could be oblivious to American actualities to the extent of saying: "How I pity all children who have not had a Doyley, a nurse who has always been there." Her autobiography is filled with so many similar notations that one realizes how much she had to overcome before she could take literature seriously.

Almost twenty years after *Sister Carrie* Logan Esarey would write in his *History of Indiana:* "From Crawfordsville also came Meredith Nicholson, one of the most widely known Indiana literary men at present. Like all literary men of Indiana he comes of good stock and enjoyed a first class education." One might dismiss this as merely "official" history, but Stuart Sherman was holding the same assumptions in 1915, in an essay in the *Nation* on "The Barbaric Naturalism of Theodore Dreiser." Objecting to the "animal behavior" of the novelist's characters, Sherman was not above attributing it to the fact that Dreiser sprang from the German rather than the Anglo-Saxon element of our "mixed population." Since Dreiser did not share in the moral ideas of our older heritage, he portrayed a "vacuum, from which the obligations of parenthood, marriage, chivalry and citizenship have been quite withdrawn. . . . Hence Mr. Dreiser's field seems curiously outside American society."

This was the kind of attack that continued against Dreiser after he had published five novels. At the outset of his career, the barriers erected by such standards might well have seemed impossible to break through. He knew what was expected from Indiana writers. Two of them were just then contributing to the immense vogue of historical romances. Charles Major's *When Knighthood Was in Flower* (1898), the romantic tale of the second marriage of "Mary of France" to Charles Brandon, was even more popular than Maurice Thompson's *Alice of Old Vincennes* (1900), whose picture of Indiana differed from Dreiser's memories not only because it dealt with frontier days. The most successful Indiana writers of Dreiser's own day would be Booth Tarkington, who had just issued *The Gentleman from Indiana* (1899), and Gene Stratton Porter. Mrs. Porter's sentimental portrayal—particularly in *Freckles* (1904) and *A Girl of the Limberlost* (1909)— of adolescent heroines in the Indiana swampland was to make her the American writer with the largest sales during the first quarter of the twentieth century, with a total of more than eight million copies.

For a writer with no sense of living tradition to protect him, such pressures of taste can be of imponderable weight. Tarkington adjusted himself easily to the current demands. The hero of his first work was the editor of a country newspaper nominally crusading against political corruption, but the milieu is handled in the tones of a light operetta. Dreiser never held any animus against Tarkington's vogue. In his later essay, "Indiana: Her Soil and Light" (1923), he linked Tarkington with Riley in their evocation "of a general geniality and sociability . . . which those who are most intimate with it are pleased to denominate 'homey' or 'folksy.'" These words have been especially prevalent in our Middle West, and another Middle Westerner, born in the same year and month as Dreiser, Vernon L. Parrington, would be more rigorous in judging the corruptions to which they are liable at the hands of authors whose smoothness is the twentieth-century face of gentility. The limitation of Tarkington's pleasant "neighborliness" is that it has little hard core of actuality. Parrington's description was accurate: "a purveyor of comfortable literature to middle-class America."

What prevented Dreiser from being seduced by the wistful charm that he knew to be the standard literary product of his native state was simply the accumulation of all the facts of his existence as we have sketched them from his birth. He could not have been a Tarkington if he had tried. He could never have acquired the lightness of touch that was at Tarkington's command from the time he was at Princeton. Dreiser was the immigrant's son from the wrong side of the tracks, who broke through the genteel tradition by no conscious intention, but by drawing on a store of experience outside the scope of the easily well-to-do—experience which formed the solid basis for all his subsequent thought.

When he began to develop Carrie Meeber's story, he remembered what had happened to one of his sisters, who had been supported in Chicago by an architect and had then felt herself much more deeply attracted by the manager of Hannah and Hogg's, a well-known eating and drinking establishment. Only later did she discover that he was married, but by then he was enough in love with her to persuade her to elope to Toronto, explaining that while drunk he had stolen fifteen thousand dollars from his employers. He was soon filled with remorse and sent back most of the money, and the owners agreed not to press the case against him. But the papers were filled with it, and the only reason the Dreisers were not involved in the scandal was that their daughter had been living under an assumed name. The couple had settled in New York where they supported themselves and two children in part by renting rooms to girls whose habits they did not scrutinize. It was to them that another sister of Dreiser's first turned when she was made pregnant by the son of a rich family who would do nothing about it. Later on, the ex-manager was to prove none too faithful to Dreiser's sister; and still later, when Dreiser was first in New York, they were having a hard time making both ends meet. Stuart Sherman might declare such material to lie "outside American society"; but, so far as Dreiser changed these details in his novel, he somewhat softened the actuality.

In her excited discovery of Chicago, Carrie is essentially Dreiser himself. Leaving her home in Wisconsin, where her father is a day laborer in a flour mill, in the summer of 1889, she approaches the city with the same "wonder and desire" that Dreiser had felt in approaching it a couple of summers earlier. For her too it is "a giant magnet." She experiences the same timidity in looking for work, the same dread of being rebuffed, and when she has landed her first job—cutting shoes—she walks to it through the "walled canyons" with the same overwhelmed sense of smallness. But the new department store windows speak to her even more importunately than they had to him, seeming to say: "You need me! You need me! You need me!" Only in this case the quotation is from Dreiser's autobiography, rather than from his novel.

But Dreiser is also Drouet, the "masher," the flashy

dresser. Or at least in his early poverty he had aspired to such clothes as he describes with intimate thoroughness when Drouet first speaks to Carrie on the train and so impresses her by his pink-and-white-striped shirt, his cuff links set with agates, the Elks' insigne on his watch-chain, his highly polished tan shoes, and his gray fedora hat. Dreiser realized that he was presenting the new manifestation of a type, "a class which at that time was first being dubbed by the slang of the day 'drummers.'" One recalls the transfixed if horrified fascination with which James was to record, in a long passage in *The American Scene*, the ubiquity of the type in our new business civilization. But Dreiser felt at home with Drouet, though he probed at once to the bottom of the man's shallow vanity. It has been noted that in Drouet's rapid "technique" for engaging Carrie's attention Dreiser is also close to one of George Ade's *Fables in Slang;* but this would appear to be a common indebtedness to American ways.

In a more profound sense Dreiser is also Hurstwood. Or rather, Hurstwood, basking in the blaze of lights and dark polished woodwork of Fitzgerald and Moy's and affable with the rich and well-placed members of his clientele, is at home in the splendor that had exercised such a tug upon Dreiser, the outsider looking in. And when later in New York, Hurstwood, no longer in his luck, begins to sag step by step down into the bottomless pit of poverty, Dreiser renders every detail of what he himself most dreaded.

The most valuable thing that Balzac had taught him was to regard the ever-changing surfaces of the new American cities as having historical importance. Dreiser could scarcely share Balzac's confidence that he was "the secretary to society"; but, having found that St. Louis or Pittsburgh was in its basic human passions no different from the great world's capital, he could hold his material in serious perspective. From his opening pages he believed that he was adding to the American record, introducing Drouet in detail "lest this order of individual should permanently pass." Impressed as he was throughout his life by the "newness" of his world, he was concerned to note such things as that Hurstwood, at his moment of crisis, just after taking the money, calls Carrie from a drugstore which contained "one of the first private telephone booths ever erected." These details are presented more baldly than they would be in more sophisticated fiction. Dreiser tells us that "At that time the department store was in its earliest form of successful operation, and there were not many. The first three in the United States, established about 1884, were in Chicago." In the light of this method of documenting his milieu, we become even more aware why Dreiser no less than Carrie was awed by the great new buildings. With an equal sense of adding to architectural history, Louis Sullivan had made, in some of these stores, the finest contributions of his functionalism.

It has often been remarked that Dreiser describes objects as though no one else had ever described them. His realization that all of his surroundings were changing continuously and rapidly served not only to detach him from them but also to make him want to seize upon them before they disappeared. This again was a great asset for his work. He recalled that not even the name "North Shore Drive," where Carrie goes riding with Hurstwood, dated back a dozen years. When he located the room of Carrie's chorus-girl friend in New York on 19th Street near Fourth Avenue, he noted that it was in "a block now given up wholly to office buildings." The lapse of time here between "then" and "now" was scarcely six years, but the fact that Dreiser could regard the change as constituting history was one of the chief reasons why his narrative has so much weight. It was why Floyd Dell would feel that Dreiser had conveyed Chicago in its full density, whereas Norris, in *The Pit*, seemed to him to have sketched it in merely as a theatrical backdrop.

Dreiser had a particular fondness for reproducing the interiors in which his characters lived. The bleakness of Carrie's sister's flat, where she stays at first, could have been selected from many memories. The apartment overlooking Union Park in which Drouet establishes Carrie is located where Dreiser had taken a room when he was a beginning reporter; but he fills it with bric-à-brac and a Brussels carpet "with gorgeous impossible flowers" which are more suitable to Carrie.

The heroine he installs here is very different from any that James or Hawthorne would have portrayed, to cite Dreiser's chief American predecessors who built novels around the characters of women. James deliberately sought out the exceptional case, an Isabel Archer or a Milly Theale, whose intense consciousness was her main resource, and his main way of measuring values. For the vibrations of her inner life took her to heights of perception and appreciation not to be reached by the crude or the unaware. Dreiser tells us at the outset that Carrie "was possessed of a mind rudimentary in its powers of observation and analysis. . . . In intuitive graces she was still crude." And he soon adds: "It must not be thought that anyone could have mistaken her for a nervous, sensitive, high-strung nature." James would have thought that a nature so lacking in the inner no less than the outer endowments which made the exceptional American girl the heiress of all the ages was not worth treating at all.

Hawthorne would have been even more puzzled by some of Dreiser's assumptions about her. Hawthorne had taken the view that Hester Prynne possessed a deeper moral nature than her Puritan judges, but he could hardly have understood Dreiser's remark that Carrie "was saved because she was hopeful." Dreiser did not think very consistently in such terms, since he had immersed Carrie in a world apart from all theological sanctions, the actual existence that he knew. Yet the title of the novel appears as *The Flesh and the Spirit* in Dreiser's first agreement with Doubleday, and it is instructive to observe the kind of allegorical pattern he had in mind. When Carrie first goes out with Drouet for an evening, Dreiser remarks that she "had no excellent home principles fixed upon her." When she accepts the salesman's further attentions, Dreiser adds that she had "only an average little conscience."

But he does not develop the struggle between forces in these conventional terms. Carrie's craving for pleasure, as represented by money and chiefly by clothes—the "things" which the fastidiousness of James's Fleda Vetch would have rejected as beneath her—is described at first as being the chief "stay" of her otherwise timid nature. Yet she is too full of "wonder" ever to be greedy. Dreiser also emphasizes that she feels "the constant drag to something better." This is suggested initially in her gradual realization that she possesses an emotional depth quite beyond the scope of the genial but egotistic drummer. Hurstwood is drawn to her by something more tender and appealing than he has found in any other woman. But Dreiser manages to crystallize her essential quality only when she gets a casual chance to appear in amateur theatricals, and unexpectedly reveals something of "the sympathetic, impressionable nature," the "pathos" of the true actress.

The potentiality glimpsed here is what Dreiser had in mind when speaking of "the spirit," as he does in several of his chapter titles. These are oddly cast in the language of magazine verse, and most of them even fall into metrical lines of eleven or twelve syllables. They throw considerable light on Dreiser's intentions. "The Lure of the Spirit: The Flesh in Pursuit" serves as the title for the two successive chapters in which Hurstwood, having witnessed her performance in Augustin Daly's *Under the Gaslight*, begins to be seriously stirred by her, and begs her to come away with him. Not knowing that he is married, she agrees on condition that he marry her. When she discovers the true state of affairs, she is "a spirit in travail." Then—in a more complex sequence than the bare facts of Dreiser's sister's situation—Hurstwood, who does not divulge that he has stolen the money, persuades her to take the train on the pretext that Drouet has been injured and is in a hospital outside the city, and only then reveals that he and she are bound for Montreal. The chapter-title reads "A Pilgrim, An Outlaw: The Spirit Detained." Dreiser continues to think of Carrie as an ignorant but slowly wakening seeker after some deeper significance in life. The first chapter after their arrival in New York is "The Kingdom of Greatness: The Pilgrim Adream." But it is only after Hurstwood has drifted far into the maelstrom of misfortune that she realizes that she must strike out for herself, and thinks of trying her lot on the stage, in a chapter headed "The Spirit Awakens: New Search for the Gate."

· 71 ·

"The flesh," as embodied in Hurstwood, is scarcely conceived as evil. In the account of Carrie's "pilgrimage," Dreiser is mainly concerned with her growth into possession of a gift, of whose existence she has been wholly unaware. She is passive rather than active, receptive rather than aggressive, and is spurred on mainly by what he calls her "helpful, urging melancholy." By the end of the book he is attributing "emotional greatness" to her of the unconscious sort that, without knowing it, can project on the stage an expression of universal longing, what Dreiser's forebears would have called *Sehnsucht*. In a brief epilogue akin to those that Balzac sometimes used, Dreiser returns to his own kind of moral judgment of her: "Not evil but that which is better, more often directs the steps of the erring. Not evil, but goodness more often allures the feeling mind unused to reason." But Carrie is not happy. Dreiser's last phrase to describe her spirit is "a harp in the wind." She has seen through her tinsel pleasures with Drouet. She has grown beyond the sphere of Hurstwood. And she finds herself essentially solitary. Dreiser takes leave of her, saying: "Know then, that for you is neither surfeit nor content. In your rocking-chair by your window dreaming, shall you long, alone. In your rocking-chair, by your window, shall you dream such happiness as you may never feel."

The core of Dreiser's problem in endowing Carrie with the reality we find in the heroines of Hawthorne and James has already been suggested by the stilted language of the chapter titles. Carrie is real when her heart is fixed on a little tan jacket with large mother-of-pearl buttons, "which was all the rage that fall." She is real, for one thing, because that final phrase comes naturally both to her and to Dreiser. Through Carrie, also, Dreiser found a register for what

Floyd Dell called "the poetry of Chicago," noting that Dreiser looked not "to see the badness of the city, nor its goodness," but "its beauty and its ugliness," and that he saw "a beauty in its ugliness." But Carrie is a much less likely vehicle for the realization at which Dreiser himself was just arriving, a realization of some of the attributes of the artistic temperament. We have a hard time believing in her "emotional greatness" as she works her way up from chorus girl to star, largely because from the moment Dreiser introduces her as "a half-equipped little knight" he has tinged his conception with banality and sentimentality. Dreiser's realm of "the spirit," in rejecting conventional standards, is so loosely defined and moreover so cluttered with clichés that it is hard to respond any longer to his sense of liberation in it. His most serious inadequacy in presenting his heroine is not what Mrs. Doubleday thought—that Carrie is too unconventional—but that she is not unconventional enough. The only way we could sense what Dreiser calls her "feeling mind" would be to see her deeply stirred, and this she never is. Her affairs with Drouet and Hurstwood are so slurred over, in instinctive accordance with what was then demanded of fiction, that they are robbed of any warmth. She is never a woman in love.

The central vitality of the novel, however Dreiser may have conceived it, lies in Hurstwood. In handling him, Dreiser seems to have learned for himself what Taine had urged upon the French novelists: "Man cannot be separated from his milieu; he leaves his imprint upon his exterior life, his house, his furniture, his affairs. . . ." Hurstwood's solid, hearty manner, just like his clothes—"not loud, not inconspicuous"—gave to Fitzgerald and Moy's the air that it needed. Its life was his life. We feel this in a redoubled sense when we see him at home, in the marriage that has become a "tinder box," his wife cold, self-centered and ambitious, his son and daughter wanting from him only money, the whole relationship becoming drier and drier and waiting only to flare into an explosion. Dreiser's emphasis here is on the opposite side of Taine's proposition. A man hardly exists apart from the milieu that nourishes him. The Hurstwood who is so affable with John L. Sullivan is driven into morose silence in such a household.

In his relationship with Carrie we feel his physical presence throughout, as we do not feel hers, even though Dreiser skirts the details of his passion. He is a man of forty, slowly but deeply aroused again to what Dreiser calls "the tragedy of affection." Another of Dreiser's basic assumptions comes out in the scene of Hurstwood's crisis, exactly midway through the book, the scene in which, having quarreled bitterly with his wife who has begun to learn of his interest in Carrie, he steals the money. We can understand why Dreiser found this scene so hard to write when we note how he transformed the bare facts. Chance is the controlling force in Dreiser's world, and chance presides over this scene. Hurstwood has had no previous thought of stealing. He has been spending the evening in the bar, drinking a little more than usual with some of the clientele because of his upset state of mind. When he steps into his office at the closing-up hour, he finds that the daytime cashier has forgotten to lock the safe, a thing that has not happened before. Glancing into the safe before locking it himself, he is surprised to see far more money than he thought Fitzgerald and Moy usually left there. He picks up the parcels of bills and mechanically counts them. Only then, "floundering among a jumble of thoughts," does temptation strike him. Here is his means of escape with Carrie. But he puts the money back in its drawer. Then he takes it out again, and feels it "so smooth, so compact, so portable." He puts it into his hand satchel. Then in a moment of revulsion, he starts to replace it in the safe; but, while the bills are in his hands, he pushes the door in his excitement and the lock clicks shut. This is the same kind of crisis that will lie at the core of *An American Tragedy*. There is no doubt about Hurstwood's desire to steal. But the act is an accident.

This central image of insecurity—and the full picture of Hurstwood's wavering back and forth is masterly—symbolizes the whole society that Dreiser evokes. It is a society in which there are no real equals, and no equilibrium, but only people moving *up* and *down*. The thoroughness with which he pursues this fact provides him with the successive links in his structure. Carrie feels herself above the "common" machine girls, but is at first dazzled by Drouet. The salesman in turn admires the substantial manager, regards Fitzgerald and Moy's as "a way-up swell place," and is attracted there by "his desire to shine among his betters." As always with Dreiser, only the massed details themselves rather than any summary of them can convey the solidity of their effect. Here is Hurstwood's knowledge of where he stands: "He knew by name, and could greet personally with a 'Well, old fellow' hundreds of actors, merchants, politicians, and the general run of successful characters about town, and it was part of his success to do so. He had a finely graduated scale of informality and friendship, which improved from the 'How do you do' addressed to the fifteen-dollar-a-week clerks and office attachés, who, by long frequenting of the place, became aware of his position, to the 'Why, old man, how are you?' which he addressed to those noted or rich individuals who knew him and were inclined to be friendly. There was a class, however, too rich, too famous, or too successful, with whom he could not attempt any familiarity of address, and with these he was professionally tactful, assuming a grave and dignified attitude, paying them the deference which would win their good feeling without in the least compromising his own bearing and opinions. There were, in the last place, a few good followers, neither rich nor poor, famous, nor yet remarkably successful, with whom he was friendly on the score of good-fellowship. These were the kind of men with whom he would converse longest and most seriously. He loved to go out and have a good time once in a while —to go to the races, the theatres, the sporting entertainments at some of the clubs. He kept a horse and neat trap, had his wife and two children, who were well established in a neat house on the North Side near Lincoln Park, and was altogether a very acceptable individual of our great American upper class—the first grade below the luxuriously rich."

The last detail is what so rankles with his family, whose eyes are fixed exclusively upon the select social world into which they have hardly begun to penetrate. It is revelatory of Dreiser that he puts his successful manager somewhat higher in the scale than he objectively belongs. The range which Dreiser can encompass from his own knowledge is from the bottom up to Hurstwood, whose domain is the kind to which Paul had introduced him. Beyond this lies the distant realm which Dreiser had not yet—had even less than Mrs. Hurstwood—perceived at first hand. It is no wonder that he was able to endow each stage of aspiration with its glowing, if frequently mean, eagerness.

With the shift to New York, Dreiser's main dramatic contrast begins slowly to establish itself. Here Carrie is to rise, while Hurstwood is gradually to sink. The chapter after their arrival begins: "Whatever a man like Hurstwood could be in Chicago, it is very evident that he would be but an inconspicuous drop in an ocean like New York." Here again Dreiser reflects on the dwarfing effect surroundings can have upon the individual: "The great create an atmosphere which reacts badly upon the small." Hurstwood must start all over again under an assumed name, and the establishment with which he gets connected is very shabby in contrast with what he had left behind him. He goes along for three years with "no apparent slope downward," but Dreiser adds that when a man of Hurstwood's age is no longer advancing, the balance is inescapably "sagging to the grave side."

Hurstwood thinks of himself as "outside a walled city," the sounds of his old life being buried more and more remotely within. His real start down begins when the owner of the land on which his bar is located decides to sell it, and Hurstwood is out of a job. He follows want ads that lead nowhere, until he is asking himself "What's the use?" Dreiser records each stage of his relapse into apathy, none of them quite perceptible to Hurstwood until it has engulfed him. There is the first time that he lounges in the lobby of a Broadway hotel instead of pursuing any further fruitless leads—an act for which he has contempt, and which he then repeats. He begins to shave every other day, every third day, every week. By then he is hardly looking at the want ads any more. In a flash of his old cocksure independence he tries his hand at a poker game, but loses. It is at this point that Carrie, frightened by the realization of where they have drifted, makes her resolution to try to get a job. Although Hurstwood feels a faint stirring of shame at her suggestion, this is overcome by his heavy lassitude. He now takes charge of the household details, and when he runs up as much of an account as one grocer will stand and then shifts to another, Dreiser remarks: "The game of a desperate man had begun."

To prove to Carrie and himself that he can still do something, he tries to work as a scab motorman during a strike, but is pulled down from his car and shot at. As he retreats again to rocking and dozing by the radiator, he dwells more and more in the past, even to hearing scraps of old conversation: "You're a dandy, Hurstwood." It is shortly after this that Carrie leaves him. The changing circumstances have long since moved them far apart. Through the people living across the hall she has met a young engineer named Ames, who talks to her about books she has never heard of, and she senses in him someone superior to Hurstwood. She never has a very coherent idea of Hurstwood's troubles. Dreiser makes the point that Hurstwood never told her about stealing the money, which he had sent back from Montreal. As he becomes completely altered from the handsome magnetic man she first knew to the drab figure brooding over his newspaper in the corner, her feelings cool. Her "heart misgave her" at walking out. "She did not want to make anyone who had been good to her feel badly." But she does not see how she can support them both and have enough left for the clothes she needs for her new career.

Dreiser effectively offsets the line of her rise against that of Hurstwood's decline. When she first attracts the critics' attention, he reads of it "down in a third-rate Bleecker

Street hotel." " 'Well, let her have it,' he said, 'I won't bother her.' " He still had that much grim pride. But there surged up before his eyes "a picture of the old, shiny, plush-covered world . . . with its lights, its ornaments, its carriages, and flowers. Ah, she was in the walled city now!" But Dreiser underscores this with irony. Carrie feels for the moment, to be sure, as though the door had opened "to an Aladdin's cave." She soon realizes that she has not really arrived anywhere. "If she wanted to do anything better or move higher she must have more—a great deal more."

Dreiser's use of such contrasting scenes in the final chapters is his most effective structural device. These chapters also contain one of the major accounts of the nature of poverty in American fiction. Melville had comprehended in *Redburn* the utter misery of the slums. But he had seen these in Liverpool; the cities of his still largely pre-industrial America had not yet yielded anything quite so menacing. But by Dreiser's time the distance had widened between the promise of Jefferson's America and the actualities of McKinley's. A perception of the change had been at the heart of Henry George's *Progress and Poverty*. It gave a peculiar urgency to his descriptions of conditions, as Bernard Shaw discerned: "Some of us regretted that he was an American, and therefore necessarily about fifty years out of date in his economics and sociology from the point of view of an older country; but only an American could have seen in a single lifetime the growth of the whole tragedy of civilization from the primitive forest clearing."

Being poor, as many Europeans have observed, can be particularly savage in a country where the *mores* of individualism consider it a disgrace, and where the official attitude is therefore tempted to pretend that poverty does not exist. The popular fiction of Dreiser's day had made it seem almost as remote as sex. In Carrie's eyes, "Everything about poverty was terrible," but its full quality enters the book only after Hurstwood is down to his last fifty cents. He gets a job in the basement of a hotel, falls sick with pneumonia, and is sent to Bellevue. From that point it is a short step to begging. One of the most effective dramatic passages is where Hurstwood, crossing Broadway one night, notices an ex-soldier who, as Dreiser remarks, "having suffered the whips and privations of our peculiar social system, had concluded that his duty to the God which he conceived lay in aiding his fellow-man." He stands on a corner soliciting money for beds, at twelve cents apiece, for a file of men who knowing that this is his nightly practice gather behind him out of the shadows. Here Dreiser can make a full contrast between the world of splendor and the world of misery, the world he had longed for and the world he dreaded, the world into which Carrie has entered and the world into which Hurstwood has sunk. Having loitered to watch a man in evening dress hand a bank note to the captain, Hurstwood edges up to the end of the line. Dreiser calls this chapter "Curious Shifts of the Poor," and one of the reasons why its details stand out with particular mastery is that he was drawing on an article he had written under the same title for *Demorest's* the year before. By introducing Hurstwood into his picture, he has given it a dynamic emotional center such as none of his articles could have.

Hurstwood's self-reliant pride is now spent. He hangs around the theater door determined that Carrie must help him. But the scene of their meeting is brief and bleak. Seeing that she is frightened at his shabby appearance, he re-

sents her even as he asks for money. She hurriedly pulls
out the contents of her purse, but it amounts to only nine
dollars in all. The next step down will be when Hurstwood
is begging and sometimes sleeping in the park, not even
aware of the sign "blazing" her name in a new show. Here
Dreiser drew again on his article for an account of the
breadlines. He knew that they were a constant feature of
the city even in times of prosperity, "when little is heard
of the unemployed." But one reason why his picture has so
much objective weight is his resistance to any tendency to
sentimentalize it. His article had concluded that "the individuals composing this driftwood are no more miserable
than others," that in fact some of them had been coarsened
by their experience to suffer less than some of their sym-
pathizers. The tap-root of Dreiser's feeling probed to a far
deeper level than any facile pity. Dorothy Dudley perceived its source when Dreiser told her that he had broken
off his manuscript because he "felt unworthy" to write
about Hurstwood's decline. "I think," she said, "that I have
not heard elsewhere such abject reverence in the face of
misery as suddenly sounded in this man's voice. If genius
is caring for human beings more than others know how to
care, then Dreiser has genius."

By now Hurstwood, to whom "life had always seemed
a precious thing," has "about concluded that the game was
up." He remembers a lodging house that has small, close
rooms with gas jets, but then reflects that he has not the
necessary fifteen cents—not even enough money to kill
himself. He begs from a gentleman coming out of a barber
shop, but when he unexpectedly gets a quarter the idea of
death fades out of his mind for the time being. But as the
worst winter weather sets in, he has less and less to eat. One

evening, so exhausted as to be hardly clear where he is going, he shambles into Broadway at 39th Street, and is face to face with a large poster of Carrie. Despite his previous resolve not to go near her again, he makes a confused lunge at the stage door. But the attendant pushes him away, and he slips and falls in the snow.

At that moment, as Hurstwood moves to his end through a succession of contrasts, Carrie is sitting in her apartment at the Waldorf, reading *Père Goriot*, which Ames had recommended to her. She is stirred by the old man's sufferings and feels sorry for the people outside in the storm. Her thoughts are interrupted by her actress friend Lola, who is standing at the window. " 'Look at that man over there,' laughed Lola, who had caught sight of someone falling down. 'How sheepish men look when they fall, don't they?' "

At that moment Drouet, who is also now located in New York, is shaking the snow from his ulster in the lobby of the Imperial. He is on his way up, in charge of a branch office. Impressed by seeing Carrie on the stage, he has brashly slurred over the fact that she left him, and has tried to renew the contact, only to learn quickly from her manner that he is out for good. On this evening he is gaily waiting for another of his endless parade of girls.

Shifting his focus once more, Dreiser turns for a page to Hurstwood's wife and daughter and the rich husband the girl has landed. They are on an eastbound train on their way to a vacation in Italy, and they now have the cold hard luster to which they had aspired. A few days later Hurstwood will go to his suicide, and not even Carrie will be aware of it.

By picking up and dropping again the threads of these

other lives in his final pages, Dreiser enforces our sensation of isolation, of a world divested of lasting human contacts. This has been accumulating from the start of the book. Once Carrie is in the city, we hear no more of her family in the country. Once she has left her sister's with Drouet, she apparently never sees her again. In New York she reflects: "I have been in this house with nine other families for over a year and I don't know a soul." Hurstwood has no relation with Shaughnessy, his three-year associate in the bar, that lasts a moment beyond the sale of the property. When Carrie has her first success and her picture in the papers, she can think of "no one she knew well enough to send them to." The continual emphasis on such details makes us realize that Dreiser conceives of the city as a jungle in a broader sense than that in which Upton Sinclair was to conceive it. Not just the poorest in the stockyards are oppressed by its naked struggle, but people on all levels who, moving up or down, are rarely able to meet and embrace as equals.

Dreiser's few basic and recurrent symbolic images serve to underscore this view. The symbol he makes most of—as we have already seen—is that of clothes, which Veblen was singling out at the same time, in *The Theory of the Leisure Class*, as giving a peculiarly representative expression of "pecuniary culture." Clothes in Dreiser are the chief means of display, of lifting a character above where he was, and by that fact above someone else. They lure—but really they separate.

His use of other images is rudimentary; he hardly thinks of them as a resource; but for this very reason there is a particular significance in a cluster that helps to create the *movement* of life as he feels it. As Carrie steps out of the train in Chicago, she is—in the last phrase of the opening chapter—"a lone figure in a tossing thoughtless sea." Other water-images heighten the sense of division. When Carrie has left the factory girls behind her, it is "as if some great tide had rolled between them." More recurrent are the phrases which project Dreiser's feeling that people are swept by forces far beyond their control. "The little shop-girl was getting into deep water. She was letting her few supports float away from her." One of the most effectively condensed similes, foreshadowing Hurstwood's disastrous career, is that which epitomizes his break with his wife: "He was like a vessel, powerful and dangerous, but rolling and floundering without sail." From this point increasingly Dreiser sees his characters as "drifting." He uses this word very often, perhaps more often than he realized, though not often enough to make the reader too conscious of it. Carrie, caught between Drouet and Hurstwood, is described as "an anchorless, storm-beaten little craft which could do absolutely nothing but drift." Later she will be "drifting" out of Hurstwood's life, as he is "drifting farther and farther into a situation which could have but one ending." By the close not only the crowd outside the flop-house are "of the class which simply floats and drifts, every wave of people washing up one, as breakers do driftwood upon a stormy shore."

Dreiser's other chief image of movement is, curiously enough, one of slow calm within the ceaseless flux. The first night at her sister's flat Carrie "drew the one small rocking-chair up to the open window, and sat looking out upon the night and streets in silent wonder." She soothes herself again and again "rocking to and fro," thinking, as in the scene with which Dreiser ends the book. Hurstwood takes similar refuge. The evening when Carrie is about to leave him, "all unconscious of his doom, he rocked and read his paper." Here Dreiser's repetition—there are more than a couple of dozen instances—probably becomes too obtrusive. But his instinctive fondness for this image is very revealing of the rhythm of experience he is projecting. The back-and-forth sway of the chair can do nothing to arrest the drift of events. Both movements are slow, but one is inexorable.

Incidentally, Dreiser's own fondness for a rocking chair, which many interviews with him noted, suggests a physical basis for the rhythm of his thoughts. The slowness with which things occur in his novels is one of the ways by which he gives them weight. He has very little of the psychologist's skill in portraying the inner life of his characters, but he is caught by an overwhelming sense of the flow of life, mysterious beyond any probing. He remarks of Hurstwood that his apathy was "almost inexplicable," and some readers are impatient at Dreiser's frequent lack of skill in detailed motivation. What he has expressed at the core of *Sister Carrie* has been well described by Charles Walcutt in the course of pointing out how basically Dreiser differs from Zola: it is "this quality of life—shifting, elusive, unaccountable—that holds our attention, rather than the spectacle of carefully analyzed forces operating under 'experimental' conditions. . . . Dreiser does not make even a pretense of controlling his conditions and discovering truths about the nature of human psychology and physiology." Where Zola's theory would "put most emphasis—on the extraction of laws about human nature—Dreiser is most uncertain and most sure that no certainty can be attained."

A novel resulting from such a reading of existence is, not

surprisingly, more impressive in its main sweep than in all its details. The same thing is true of Dreiser's style. Emerson found Whitman's language a strange "mixture of the *Bhagvat-Geeta* and the *New York Herald*." Dreiser's mixture was even stranger since his journalistic usages were not counterbalanced by any pure body of poetry or scripture. The passages conveying the "glamor" of the city as Carrie felt it, in a chrome equivalent of *The Arabian Nights*, are in a sense accidental rather than intentional. He is not deliberately using Carrie as a register, as a later master of our city speech might have. He himself felt the city in the same way, but when he strove for effect he merely fell into the stilted usages of magazine fiction: "Thus was Carrie's name bandied about in the most frivolous and gay of places, and that also when the little toiler was bemoaning her narrow lot." If one began enumerating the fancy clichés that spatter his pages—"lightsome," "halcyon," "prancing pair of bays," "airy grace"—one might conclude that this writer could not possibly break through to freshness. But what bothered his first reviewers was the opposite tendency, the extent to which Dreiser introduced words from his own conversation: "flashy," "nobby," "truly swell saloon," "dress suit affair." Objections on these grounds led him to say (at the time of the book's reissue in 1907): "To sit up and criticize me for saying 'vest' instead of 'waistcoat'; to talk about my splitting the infinitive and using vulgar commonplaces here and there, when the tragedy of a man's life is being displayed, is silly. . . . It makes me feel that American criticism is the joke that English authorities maintain it to be."

But once more this partly dodges the question, and also fails to do justice to the firm body of what he achieved.

Charges of clumsiness have been repeated against him so often that they have obscured the many passages where, like the journeyman painter, he has a mastery of the plain style. When his mind was most absorbed with what he had to say, the flourishes of the feature-writer fell away, as did also the cumbersome, only half-accurate abstract terms ("affectional," "actualities"). Then he could write long passages where nothing is striking except the total effect. He is at his rare best in conveying the first understated rift between Hurstwood and Carrie, with everything keyed down to the neutral phrases that passed between them over the supper table. Or in conveying the brutal blankness of Hurstwood's separation from his partner Shaughnessy, or the pitiful blankness of the scene where Hurstwood begs from Carrie. Or in the entire chapter dealing with the streetcar strike, or in that one on the "curious shifts" of the poor. It is impossible to suggest the power of these in brief quotations, or in anything short of the whole. The same would be true of the pages in which Hurstwood moves towards his end through a winter evening, which is portrayed in uniform tones of "somber" and "thickening" air, "dirty store fronts," and "dingy brown" snow. This is the close of the passage, after Hurstwood has paid his fifteen cents and gone to his small room:

"Now he began leisurely to take off his clothes, but stopped first with his coat, and tucked it along the crack under the door. His vest he arranged in the same place. His old wet, cracked hat he laid softly upon the table. Then he pulled off his shoes and and lay down.

"It seemed as if he thought a while, for now he rose and turned the gas out, standing calmly in the blackness, hidden from view. After a few moments, in which he reviewed nothing, but merely hesitated, he turned the gas on again, but applied no match. Even then he stood there, hidden wholly in the kindness that is night, while the uprising fumes filled the room. When the odour reached his nostrils, he quit his attitude and fumbled for the bed.

" 'What's the use?' he said weakly, as he stretched himself to rest."

There are no words here for ornament, and the predominating monosyllables are right for the basic simplicity. The only three-syllabled word in the first paragraph is one that calls attention to Dreiser's tragic irony. His resolve taken, Hurstwood can be "leisurely," though his leisure will be only in the "rest" of death. Dreiser's feeling for the dignity of man, even at the last extreme, comes through in Hurstwood's calmness. But the key-word in bringing out Dreiser's attitude towards life is "kindness." Even at its worst, life contains something which he, with full compassion for his beaten hero, will not reject, but will embrace with tenderness.

What *Sister Carrie* brought into American literature in 1900 may be pointed up further by a few comparisons. The difference in scope between Howells and Dreiser may be observed most concretely by turning back to the account of the streetcar strike that Howells introduced into *A Hazard of New Fortunes* (1890), the first of his novels to deal with New York. Writing a preface for it twenty years later, Howells was quite right in believing this novel to have become his "most vital" in response to his "quickened interest" in the life about him in the vast city in which he had just settled. He also had the opportunity of studying a strike at first hand, with the result that his story "began to find its way to issues nobler and larger than those of the love-affairs common to fiction."

He used the strike in his novel as a double means of bringing his plot to a climax, and of concentrating the social views of his chief characters. The hero, March, a liberal magazine-editor, is the temperate observer who sounds the theme that "the roads have rights and the strikers have rights, but the public has no rights at all." Old Dryfoos, the German-American who has struck it rich in Pennsylvania oil, says, "If I had my way I'd have a lot of those vagabonds hung." The main tension in the book is between Dryfoos and his radical religious son, Conrad, who now outrages his father by being sympathetic with the strikers —though taking the position that strikes, like all violence, are wrong. Miss Vance, the rich girl who works for the cause of the poor, blames her own class, but thinks that someone should point out to the strikers the futility of their effort and persuade them to stop. Moved by her words, Conrad walks over towards the West Side, and arrives just at the moment of an outbreak of violence—which March also witnesses. The old radical, Lindau (who had lost his hand in our Civil War), is being clubbed by a policeman. Conrad tries to come to his aid, but is shot by a stray bullet and instantly killed. The stump of Lindau's arm is so badly shattered that it has to be amputated, and he dies from the shock.

Howells's scene of crisis is much too melodramatic to be effective in his otherwise quiet book. But there is no question that, as a reader of Henry George and Edward Bellamy, he was able to perceive several of the leading issues that came to the surface through a strike. Dreiser presented far fewer issues. The strike simply offered Hurstwood a chance of proving that he "was not down yet." When he first read about it in the papers, he sympathized with the men's demands; "indeed, it is a question whether he did not always sympathize with them to the end, belie him as his actions might." But the fact that Hurstwood—and Dreiser —have known the brutal necessity of having a job seems to have brought all the material much closer. Howells, like March, has conscientiously observed a strike. Dreiser has virtually enacted one.

In part this is a matter of more incisive handling. In a single sentence he cuts through the assumptions of Howells's liberals: "There was nothing so helpful to the companies as peaceful methods." Yet Dreiser is not writing as a radical. He is only drawing on the store of what he began to know, without realizing it, when he watched that Chicago strike at sixteen. His conversation, which can sometimes be fumbling, is here compact and right. It is what he has heard for himself, as well as what he read in the papers at the time of another strike during his first winter in New York. "A poor man ain't nowhere. You could starve, by God, right in the streets, and there ain't most no one would help you." An effective touch of irony comes when the strikers have stopped the car Hurstwood is running, and their leader says: "Come off the car, pardner. . . . We're all working men, like yourself." The fact that Hurstwood—and Dreiser —had not been working men adds detachment to their involvement, and the combination makes for objective weight.

We live through the experience with Hurstwood, until he has had enough and quits. The strike has not served Dreiser, as it did Howells, to get away from the materials of conventional fiction. It is of a piece with the rest of his book. In the dozen chapters following Conrad's death Howells diffused his energies in tying up all the strands of his plot, even taking Conrad's sister to Europe to marry a French nobleman. Dreiser did not have to escape from the conventional love affairs expected by Howells's audience; he had rejected them before he began. And the fact that it would not have occurred to him to describe the strike issues as "noble"—a word particularly dear to the genteel tradition and scarcely in Dreiser's vocabulary—enabled him to portray its savage reality. We can comprehend now how far he saw into his "picture of conditions," as we can also perceive the rudimentary but forceful "craftsmanship" that empowered him to present it in its essential lights and darks.

A comparison with Dreiser's contemporaries is also illuminating. *McTeague* is Norris's best book, with its scenes "indigenous" to San Francisco, as Dreiser noted, and with all its author's fresh vigor involved in portraying his naturalistic animal hero. But the account of McTeague's decline into poverty breaks out of control in the highly melodramatic scene in which he murders his estranged wife. And when, after his flight into Death Valley, he perishes of thirst, handcuffed to the dead body of his pursuer, we are left with the kind of immature image of violence which was Norris's besetting weakness.

There is, naturally enough, a similar immaturity in Crane's first book, undertaken when he was hardly past twenty. *Maggie* shocked many of its first readers as being too frank and too sordid. It now appears both forced and callow. Its plot is the conventional one of seduction, betrayal, and suicide. Crane declared the Bowery to be the most interesting part of New York, but it is no detraction from his daring experiments with words to call this account an outsider's job. When he writes, "In the mingled light and gloom of an adjacent park, a handful of wet wanderers, in attitudes of chronic dejection, were scattered among the benches," he suggests his essential kinship with the impressionistic painters. But he gives little sense of the human beings in his scene. Except in the page or two when Maggie walks through the darkness to the river, she is far less realized even than Carrie. Her seducer, the red-haired bartender Pete, behaves much more like a high-school boy. A single sentence describing Maggie's mother may illustrate Crane's lack of touch with his material: "With lurid face and tossing hair she cursed and destroyed furniture all Friday afternoon." She is repeatedly described as "shrieking," "howling," "floundering," "screeching," "glaring," "raving," to the point that she becomes—quite contrary to Crane's intention—merely a comic grotesque. Her recurrent destruction of furniture overlooks a fact that Dreiser would not have forgotten, that there would have been no money to replace it. Crane had little comprehension of "the curious shifts of the poor." He was a natural-born writer, as Dreiser was not. When he achieved greater control over his flair for striking phrases, he could sustain the psychological *tour de force* of *The Red Badge of Courage*, and of the even more brilliantly wrought shorter pieces, "The Open Boat" and "The Blue Hotel." But his sphere was not the somber enduring humanity of a Hurstwood. With that figure Dreiser began his chief contribution to American literature.

Ten Years in the Desert

THE suppression of *Sister Carrie* became, particularly in the nineteen-twenties, a legend with respect to the problem of the artist in America. As told and retold after Mencken, perhaps some of its details got exaggerated; perhaps, for example, Mrs. Doubleday's role was overestimated. Her husband, who was abroad when the manuscript was accepted, may easily have pronounced it "an immoral book" even without her shocked protest at the thought of its bearing the firm's imprint. Confronted with the publisher's eagerness to cancel the contract, Dreiser might have taken the book to another house. But without any financial margin he could think of no better course than stubbornly to insist that the reluctant firm stand by its agreement. In any case, on legal advice it did fulfill the bare letter of the contract; the book was issued in a thousand copies, though with no advertising at all.

The reviews were not all unfavorable. A high proportion took the position that it was "unpleasant" or "not elevating mental food," or went on to object that "there is no strong or noble nature in the book; neither is there any lady or gentleman. . . . If only Carrie could be more like Trilby!"

But one reviewer who said, "You would never dream of recommending it to another person to read," had to conclude that "the fact remains that as a work of literature and the philosophy of human life it comes within sight of greatness." Still another said: "The characters are so genuine that they produce that queer feeling . . . one sometimes gets from listening to a phonograph. You are certain that the human beings must lie just a little back of the talk." But Dreiser's first real champion was William Marion Reedy of St. Louis, whose *Mirror* was later to encourage Masters and Sandburg. He had no hesitation in declaring *Sister Carrie* "a tip-top novel." The English reviewers were in the main impressed by this American's being "untrammeled by any concession to convention or tradition, literary or social." Arnold Bennett was soon to say that here was "perhaps the great American novel."

With no advertising, however, the sale was poor—hardly six hundred and fifty copies, including those sent out by Norris for review. Dreiser did not net even a hundred dollars. At this point the story usually stops. What has been far less known is the slowly cumulative effect of this whole experience upon him. A sense of futility deepened into a depression and a breakdown which led almost to suicide. Any sustained work became impossible for him for over three years. A decade would elapse before he would dare trust himself again to fiction.

At the time of the acceptance of *Sister Carrie* he already had ideas for two more novels. He referred to these as *The Transgressor* and *The Rake*, which indicates a growing habit of thinking of his subjects as typifications that he would then imbed in details. *The Transgressor* was finally to be known as *Jennie Gerhardt*. *The Rake*, according to notes left among Dreiser's manuscripts, was to have been based on a famous murder trial in 1899-1900, in which Roland Molineux, gentleman sportsman, was first sentenced to death, and some four years later retried and acquitted, on the charge of sending poison to a fellow member of the Knickerbocker Athletic Club in New York City. Dreiser's sketches for his opening chapters reveal what his emphasis would have been. They place his hero, Ansley Bellinger, in his boyhood in New York, halfway in the scale between rich and poor, but with his mind consumed by images of the city's wealth. They foreshadow, if in a very different form, some of the issues with which Dreiser was to be concerned in *An American Tragedy*.

After Doubleday's treatment of *Sister Carrie*, other publishers expressed only indifference to these further projects, though Dreiser did manage to get a small advance on *The Transgressor* from the little-known firm of J. F. Taylor. By the summer of 1901 he was beginning to feel very insecure psychologically, but he turned his thoughts temporarily away from himself by making two character sketches of men far removed from his problems. "A True Patriarch" was based on his wife's father, whom he likened to Whitman in his abundant confidence. "A Doer of the Word," growing out of his conversations with a rural character he met during a month with Arthur Henry at Noank, Connecticut, voiced Dreiser's sense of surprised discovery that the religious life could be real.

Back in New York he was so pressed for money that he and his wife had to give up their small apartment near Central Park, and she returned to Missouri for the winter. The unhappy facts of their marriage were to be written out at length in *The "Genius,"* and more affectingly in a short story, "Married." This was one of the stories that so moved Sherwood Anderson by its honesty. It represented the wife no less sympathetically than the husband. But it found no basis for compatibility in her simple devotion which felt out of place and suspicious among his more complex and varied interests. Dreiser and his wife tried to escape this dilemma by what he called "a prolonged riot of indulgence between them." This did not serve to hold them together, though their final separation was still some years away.

In the early winter he joined her on her father's farm, but could not settle to writing about Jennie Gerhardt there. Sallie seemed increasingly uncomprehending of his work, and he felt that he had to be free for it. But when he tried to get along on his own in a cheaper New York apartment (overlooking the East River and what was then called Blackwell's Island), he had to turn again to articles to support himself. He wrote more about the poor, this time about the immigrants in the tenements, with the harsh conclusion that "nearly the only ideal that is set before these strugglers . . . is the one of getting money," that they "are inoculated in infancy with the doctrine that wealth is all—the shabbiest and most degrading doctrine that can be impressed upon anyone."

What began to overtake him now was "the most dreadful and inhibiting and destroying of all forms of poverty . . . poverty of mind." The full weight of his discouragement over the fate of his novel had slowly sunk down upon him. The bleak material of his articles came to be more than he could stand. It was too close to him, like the view out of his window of the prison and the hospital for the insane. He could not bear to write about it any more. But he soon found that he could not write about anything else either.

The futility, not just of his own effort, but of all effort, settled in on him. Life seemed "an endless chain without meaning."

Trying to get a grip on himself, he left New York for Roanoke, Virginia, which he had visited before his marriage. But he felt no better there. More and more restless, he walked through Virginia and Delaware to Philadelphia. With no fixed purpose he lingered in that city for six months, declining ever deeper into melancholy. He had reached the stage where he was ashamed to see his family or his friends. He was haunted by premonitions, but he could get no clear diagnosis of his state from any doctor he could afford. He finished a few scattered pieces for Philadelphia papers, but had to write Taylor that he could not continue *The Transgressor*, and would try to repay the advance. He finally returned to New York as his "only home," and took a cheap room in Brooklyn. "Across the water was the great city in which I had hoped to attract so much attention."

Dreiser spoke of this time as one when "there were furies between me and the way I would go." After he had found his way back to health, he wrote out a detailed account of what had happened to him, as though to complete his exorcism of it: "All that is, now passes before me a rich, varied and beautiful possession. I have fought a battle for the right to live and for the present, musing with stilled nerves and a serene gaze, I am the victor.

"For three years preceding the writing of this statement I was a victim of neurasthenia. For that period I endured all the pains, all dreads, all the agonies of one whose mind is under a cloud."

To an extraordinary degree he was re-enacting that aspect of Hurstwood's numb apathy which he had most dreaded writing about. It should be added, as a relevant coincidence, that in these same years Edwin Arlington Robinson—the most searching tragic poet of Dreiser's generation—was making, while clinging to a marginal job as a New York subway inspector, his crucial struggle against the furies of poverty and despair.

Like Hurstwood, Dreiser found that "the approach of actual want was such an insidious thing that I really did not perceive how far I was getting into the depths before I was fairly caught and unable to extricate myself." He would start out to look for a job, and would then be overcome by the weary certainty of refusal. He even thought of trying the streetcar lines; but when he reached the office he "could not find the heart to go in." Unlike Hurstwood, he had been a writer, "but now my power to write was taken away from me."

He moved to a smaller room, the smallest in which he had ever lived. "The period of the occupancy of this chamber proved unquestionably the dreariest of my life. It combined the various qualities of sickness, want, friendlessness and limitation which go to make up the lowest state of life, this side of suicide." He passed night after night of insomnia. "It seemed sometimes that if I did not get sleep pretty soon I would go mad. But I did not."

There came upon him the sensation that he had become two persons: "One of these was a tall, thin greedy individual who had struggled and thought always for himself and how he should prosper, but was now in a corner and could not get out, and the other was a silent, philosophical soul who was standing by him watching him in his efforts and taking an indifferent interest in his failures."

More pronounced hallucinations followed. He would hear the slow footfalls of someone approaching, he would feel a hand "reconnoitring" his pillow. "I also had the strangest desire to turn around, as if I must go in a circle whether I would or no, which was nothing more nor less than pure insanity." One form this took was that when sitting in a chair he would keep readjusting it, trying to bring himself into correct alignment with something, continually turning to the right, until he had brought himself all the way around. "In this crisis I do not know what would have become of me if it had not been for the presence of the sane conservative oversoul which I have mentioned, the other person who sat in judgment on me and all that I did and seemed to brood apart like another person, over my fate. This other person was a more courageous individual than I —cold, immovable, indifferent—for he did not trouble over my worries in the least. Always he was with me when I stood outside shop doors and hesitated to go in, when I waited at the ferry wondering whether I could afford the few pennies that it would take to carry me across, when I wandered from magazine room to magazine room trying to get a place, and when I returned to the bleak room and he laughed at me as I stared hopelessly out of the window. He was at my bedside during the long hours of the night where I tossed and tumbled and he rose with me in the morning only to dog me patiently through another day. He was not sorry for me. He was not ashamed of me. He seemed rather to look upon me as I looked upon those flies I had so often seen caught in the paste of a paper, or the moths that I watched turning about my lamp and burning their wings. He was not exactly cruel. He was not kind. He seemed to look upon me as some poor, disturbed and rather distraught creature who really did not deserve much to live and who did not really deserve to die. He was very wise and sane and I had great faith in him.

"What the presence of this superior consciousness meant to me I can hardly say. It was my refuge and my salvation. He would not go crazy. In all probability he would bring me through. Something would happen."

What happened first was a still deeper descent into a feeling of "the vastness, the indifference, the desolation of the world." One night, when he no longer had even the dollar and a half to meet his next week's rent, he started down to the river. While he was hovering there on the edge, a boatman came up and asked him if he wanted a ride across to Towanda. Dreiser answered out of his surprise: "Why should you want me to go on your boat?" "I thought maybe you were trying to run away from your wife." At the incongruity of this Dreiser laughed, and the spell was broken.

That night he slept a little, and his sundered nature came back together enough to let him escape from his apathy, and to try once again to rescue himself. He recalled having heard that the passenger agent of the New York Central had helped out literary men who were in need of jobs, and decided to apply there. He cited his poor health, and asked for outdoor work. His interviewer had, of course, no notion of the depth of his need, and suggested that he might find benefit in using a Whitely exerciser. When Dreiser went out through the anteroom, his last loaf of bread, which he had embarrassedly left on a window-ledge, was gone. But he had the promise of a position on the road.

He was not to go to work there just yet. Paul had finally discovered where he was, and, taking in at a glance his depleted state, broke through his self-centered aloofness. He insisted on sending him to a sanitarium, run by Paul's friend the old retired wrestling champion, Muldoon. Most of the other patients were rich men who had damaged their health by dissipation, and Dreiser came to "the bitterest view of humanity" he had ever had through contemplating their sheer "materiality." Muldoon was a human tiger, with contempt for weakness of any kind, but his fierce vitality was tonic, and the regimen of Spartan exercise through which he put Dreiser began to restore his nervous equilibrium. After several weeks there he was in so much better shape that, in the early summer of 1903, he could start working in the railroad yard at Spuyten Duyvil on the Hudson.

Here he responded to another strong personality, Mike Burke, the section foreman. He was to include Mike in *Twelve Men* as "The Mighty Rourke," as he included Muldoon as "Culhane, the Solid Man." Working as Burke's clerical assistant, Dreiser at first thought of Burke as "an Irish brute," but as he watched him with his Italian gang he realized that beneath Burke's excited harrying of them was a real devotion, like that of a sheep dog to his flock. "It was delicious to watch him," Dreiser wrote, and managed to evoke this feeling in what is probably the best of his short portraits. He catches Burke's quality of warm humanity, "something intimate and fatherly." He also suggests how—in the midst of his own still depressing thoughts that he had "permanently fallen," and that he "would never be able to rise above these miserable circumstances again"— Burke's simple organic grasp of actualities began to "heal" him, to teach him once again how to live. At first Dreiser had not liked the men; they struck him as "contentious and sullen." They came from below his usual orbit, as the men at the sanitarium had come from above it. But Burke helped him to approach closer to them, and he long remembered the fervor with which one of them said: "America fine. No lika any place but America."

One day in the fall he felt impelled to jot down on his pad of O.K. blanks some loosely rhythmical lines about the somber beauty of November. Heartened by their acceptance by a magazine—even though for only five dollars and with the statement that it could use very little poetry—he felt that he was ready to face the city once more. Availing himself of some of his other magazine connections, he secured a position as assistant feature editor of Munsey's *Daily News*, and was immersed again in the flow of existence. He had a new and deepened desire to read further in history and philosophy. But he did not dare trust himself to writing fiction. The material he knew best might again prove too painful for him to dwell upon. The overwhelming insecurity of his prospects as a writer was more than he could stand.

The next half-dozen years constitute the most unlikely chapter in the life of a man who was to hold to the authenticity of naturalism. He worked his way up from thirty-five dollars a week to ten thousand a year as an editor of magazines whose standards were everything that he resisted in his own fiction. When Munsey soon discontinued his Sunday feature section, Dreiser was hired by Street & Smith to cut fiction for their *Popular Magazine*, and soon afterward was made editor of *Smith's Magazine*. In the first capacity, he said, his main job was doubling the output by cutting adventure novels in half, supplying a climax for the first half and a new beginning for the second. He could now afford to set up an apartment with his wife, after a separation of two years and a half. He also paid back the advance on *The Transgressor*.

By the spring of 1906 he had moved on to be managing editor of *The Broadway Magazine*, where his assignment was to transform a "white light" monthly into a "home" one. As though wiping out of his mind everything that he cared for, he said that "the heavy is never the effective or the important," and promised a magazine that would not be "a drain on your intellectual resources to appreciate." He turned out to have an unexpected flair for this role, his employer was greatly impressed by his "marvellous objective mind," and the circulation rose rapidly from twelve thousand to over a hundred thousand.

Only a year later he was offered the direction of the Butterick "trio"—*The Designer, The New Idea Woman's Magazine,* and especially *The Delineator:* all issued primarily to distribute Butterick dress patterns, so that we have the odd circumstance of Carrie's creator working in a realm that would greatly have appealed to her. With a staff of thirty-two under him, he was incessantly busy—in close touch with the culinary editor, the children's editor, the interior-decoration editor. He solicited popular serials, built up the correspondence columns, and scrutinized the magazines' entire contents, including fashion articles: "Fêtes and Frocks in Paris" and "Dressing on Dimes." He became known as "an idea-man," and an occasional editorial touched, if remotely, on one of his old interests, such as "The Romance of the Unexplainable." But he accepted all the restrictions of a magazine in which none of his own stories could have appeared, including the taboos against any illustration showing a wine glass on a table or a woman with a cigarette in her hand. He even went to the length of writing to one contributor: "We like realism, but it must be tinged with sufficient idealism to make it all of a truly uplifting character. Our field in this respect is limited by the same limitations which govern the well-regulated home. We cannot admit stories which deal with false or immoral relations, or which point a false moral, or which deal with things degrading, such as drunkenness. . . . The fine side of things—the idealistic—is the answer for us, and we find really splendid material within these limitations."

Dorothy Dudley concluded of this period: "So Dreiser made the magazines. He was on the inside now among the money makers. He could exclude as he had often been excluded. He was a procurer among the prostitutes of literature." It is astonishing that any of his genuine quality survived.

In 1907 *Sister Carrie* was taken over by the newly started firm of B. W. Dodge and reissued with commendations from Reedy, Brand Whitlock, Hamlin Garland, and others. But Dreiser told an interviewer that he was too busy to work on another novel. What seems to have helped most to keep him alive was his never-flagging interest in personalities; and since *The Delineator* was allowed to reflect the muckraking movement in a mild way, several lively journalists came to his office. Young Sinclair Lewis reported that he looked "more like a wholesale hardware merchant than a properly hollow-cheeked realist." But others were more awed by his enormous paneled office, by the distant armchair from which he looked down upon them through his pince-nez with their black ribbon. William Lengel, who was his secretary, remembered his first impression: "His hair was the color of wet straw. His forehead was high and broad. He had bushy eyebrows and one eye was set lower than the other, a curious gray-blue—in one, a cast, which made it difficult to tell which eye was fixed on you. A large well-shaped nose, and a large, full-lipped and strangely misshapen mouth. He wore a stiff-looking herringbone suit. . . . Not as I had expected an editor to look. More like a college professor. . . . He was rude, ruthless, abrupt. . . . When he gave orders, he tried to be jovial, bantering. But those curious eyes and that twisted mouth made his attempted lightness seem arrogant and dictatorial." Yet Lengel came to be devoted to him, and added, "A dynamo himself, he charged and vitalized the staff." He believed that the main reason for Dreiser's success as an editor was that "he loved the surge of life around him."

One interview symbolizes this period in Dreiser's career. He had negotiated with a Baltimore physician, Leonard Hirshberg, for a series of articles on child-care, and the doctor arranged for his ghost-writer to come on for a conference. This was Dreiser's memory of it, in 1925: "There appeared in my office a taut, ruddy, blue-eyed, snub-nosed youth of twenty-eight or nine whose brisk gait and ingratiating smile proved to be at once enormously intriguing and amusing. I had, for some reason not connected with his basic mentality you may be sure, the sense of a small town roisterer or a college sophomore of the crudest and yet most disturbing charm and impishness, who, for some reason, had strayed into the field of letters. More than anything else he reminded me of a spoiled and petted and possibly over-financed brewer's or wholesale grocer's son who was out for a lark. With the sang-froid of a Caesar or a Napoleon he made himself comfortable in a large and impressive chair which was designed primarily to reduce the over-confidence of the average beginner. And from that particular and unintended vantage point he beamed on me with the confidence of a smirking fox about to devour a chicken. So I was the editor of the Butterick Publications. He had been told about me. However, in spite of *Sister Carrie*, I doubt if he had ever heard of me before this. After studying him in that almost arch-episcopal setting which the chair provided, I began to laugh. 'Well, well,' I said, 'if it isn't Anheuser's own brightest boy out to see the town.' And with that unfailing readiness for any nonsensical flight that has always characterized him, he proceeded to insist that this was true. 'Certainly he *was* Baltimore's richest brewer's son and the yellow shoes and bright tie he was wearing were characteristic of the jack-dandies and rowdy-dows of his native town. Why not? What else did I expect? His father brewed the best beer in the world.' All thought of the original purpose of the conference was at once dismissed and instead we proceeded to palaver and yoo-hoo anent the more general phases and ridiculosities of life, with the result that an understanding based on a mutual liking was established, and from then on I counted him among those whom I most prized—temperamentally as well as intellectually. And to this day, despite various disagreements, that mood has never varied."

This passage strikes the prevailing tone of the relationship between Dreiser and Mencken, who stimulated one phase of Dreiser's nature as no one else did. A lively stream of letters was to begin to flow from Baltimore, bearing signatures ranging from "Aloysius Hohenzollern" to "Jesus Baumgarten," and calling out more lumbering answers in the same vein from "Billy the Oysterman" or "Cotton Mather." Presently Dreiser was to suggest Mencken for a position on *The Smart Set*, and to read with growing interest his book on Nietzsche. It is hard to say which one was farther from his proper work: Mencken as the writer of an article on "When Baby Has Diphtheria," or Dreiser as the one who solicited the article.

When Dreiser got control of still another magazine, *The Bohemian*, for a few months in 1909, he wrote Mencken: "I want bright stuff. I want humor. And above all I want knowledge of life *as it is*, broad, simple, good-natured." But he had been sufficiently contaminated by his surroundings to add that he did not want "any tainted fiction." When this magazine failed, he began to grow restless at Butterick's, though his salary was still rising. He stayed there through another year, and then the job blew up as the result of an affair with the daughter of a woman in the Butterick organization, who denounced him in the office and to his wife. Young Lengel looked upon him as "a broken man." But Dreiser could write to a colleague that he did not regret his resignation since "the big work was done here," quite with the air of having believed in its bigness. Huneker cut through to the truth when he wrote: "If you, Theodore Dreiser, could or would return to your old field, the gain for our literature would be something worth while."

Dreiser began to see his editorial days in some perspective only as he looked back at them a few years later: "It was pathetic, as I look at it now, the things we were trying to do and the conditions under which we were trying to do them—the raw commercial force and theory which underlay the whole thing, the necessity of explaining and fighting for so much that one should not, as I saw it then, have to argue over at all. . . . My own experience with *Sister Carrie*, as well as the fierce opposition or chilling indifference which, as I saw, overtook all those who attempted anything even partially serious in America, was enough to make me believe that the world took anything even slightly approximating the truth as one of the rankest and most criminal offenses possible. One dared not talk out loud, one dared not report life as it was, as one lived it."

The Large, Truthful Lines
of Life

DREISER was to publish seven books in the next
six years: four long novels, two travel books, and
a collection of plays. On first leaving Butterick's
he was very uncertain what to do, and wrote Mencken: "I
am considering several good things. My conscience hurts
me a little though, for first off I should finish my book. And
I may." As soon as he made the plunge and trusted himself
again to the story of Jennie Gerhardt, he experienced a
great welling up of the creative energy that had been
dammed off for so long.

From his years as an editor he preserved practically
nothing, though he tried now without success to find
a publisher for his city sketches, under the title *Idylls of
the Poor*, many of which dated from before his breakdown.
He resumed his work in isolation. Paul had died in 1906,
from a burst blood-vessel. Dreiser and Arthur Henry had
drifted apart; as Dorothy Dudley remarked, Dreiser had
"a gift for estrangement nearly equal to his gift for engage-
ment." As an aftermath of the affair that had cost him his
job, he and his wife had again separated. In the view of one

of his friends, he "was subject to fits of terrible depression, impossible to live with, I should think." He took a room on Riverside Drive, and returned to his manuscript. He wrote on it through the winter, adapting for his desk the case of an old square piano once owned by Paul. The book was accepted by Harper in the spring and came out in the fall of 1911.

What had been happening in American fiction during the decade since he had left it? Crane had died from tuberculosis in the year in which *Sister Carrie* appeared, and Norris from a ruptured appendix only two years later. Neither Garland nor Fuller had gone beyond their early work. Among the popular successes were the short stories of O. Henry and the novels of Winston Churchill, who had turned from historical fiction to some of the themes stressed by the muckrakers—the roles played by the railroad lobby and the political bosses. David Graham Phillips, Robert Herrick, and several others were writing novels of big business, to which genre Dreiser would turn in *The Financier*. The socialist fiction of Jack London and Upton Sinclair was also having a considerable vogue, but Dreiser seems never to have been drawn to London, and his interest in Sinclair did not really ripen until many years later when Dreiser himself became involved with radical politics.

The more deliberate artists were finding their audience very slowly. Most of them at this period were women, and the three new figures after Edith Wharton were all three or four years younger than Dreiser. Ellen Glasgow knew what she was about from the time her first social studies of Virginia began to appear at the turn of the century, but her critical success hardly came until the nineteen-twenties. She was not attracted by the "severely regimented" realism of

Howells, and added: "I had not revolted from the Southern sentimental fallacy in order to submit myself to the tyranny of the Northern genteel tradition." She admired James, but felt "not the slightest disposition to imitate him." She learned much, as he had done, from the modern French masters. So also did Willa Cather, who was advised by her first great admiration, Sarah Orne Jewett, to study Flaubert's style. But Miss Cather arrived at maturity late, and her first novel, *Alexander's Bridge*, was not published until the year after *Jennie Gerhardt*. Gertrude Stein had issued *Three Lives* in a small edition in 1909, though Dreiser was doubtless unaware of it. With almost as sure a possession of realistic surfaces as Maupassant, and with a grasp of psychology which she owed in part to her teacher, William James, she shared, if only at this time, in a subject matter like Dreiser's. But her Melanctha, and "the good" Anna, and "the gentle" Lena, are seen as servant girls with a detachment that would have been impossible to him. In the same year as *Jennie Gerhardt*, Edith Wharton, turning away from the New York material that was her surest possession to rural New England, produced in *Ethan Frome* the kind of spare, stylized piece of craftsmanship which was everything that Dreiser never mastered.

He picked up where he had left off. He gives no sign of knowing anything more about other more complex kinds of fiction. What is far more remarkable is that his own writing had not been softened or made slick by the standards he had accepted as an editor. Mencken was to praise Dreiser's resistance, tough as an elephant's hide, to whatever did not belong to his own nature. Even in the midst of his magazine work he had said, on the reissue of *Sister Carrie*: "Life is a tragedy. . . . The infinite suffering and deprivation of great masses of men and women upon whom existence has been thrust unasked appals me." Now, in an interview after *Jennie Gerhardt* he reaffirmed: "My own ambition is to represent my world, to conform to the large, truthful lines of life."

Even the theme of his second novel is closely akin to that of his first. The seduction of Jennie is not regarded as evil. Senator Brander is deeply stirred by her beauty, as she comes week by week to his hotel room, delivering laundry for her mother. He senses an unusual richness in her unformed nature, and, after making love to her, intends to marry her, but is prevented by his sudden illness and death. Dreiser's view of Jennie throughout the remainder of the book is of a character more generous and more spiritual than that achieved by the society which excludes her and her illegitimate child. He seems to have had to struggle to hold to the simple clarity of his design. In the first draft he had Jennie marry Lester Kane, the rich man whose mistress she became for many years; but in the revision Lester yields to the pressures of society and finally breaks off his relations with her to make the correct marriage expected of him. (Dreiser also ended his manuscript with a moralizing epilogue, which Huneker advised him to cut out; but it appeared in all issues of the first edition, though it was dropped from the reprint of the nineteen-twenties.) In dealing with passion Dreiser is, as before, very conventional, and all the love passages are slurred over.

For the most part he was writing, once again, out of what he knew best. What he seems to have fallen into by instinct in *Sister Carrie* is now established as a feature of his fiction. He was never to display much invention, which indicates a severe limitation to his imaginative resources. "It is so hard for us to know what we have not seen," he observed. "It is so difficult for us to feel what we have not experienced." The second of these observations continued to be a main source of strength within his limitations, since, writing out of what he himself had experienced, he could make others feel it. He did not fall into mechanical recall, and he offset his lack of invention with a gift for selection and massive rearrangement.

The opening situation he chose again approximated that of one of his sisters, but Jennie's character was based far more on what he had loved most in his mother. The whole book gives the sense of being solidly planted in the Middle West, though the Columbus, Ohio, where it starts and for the rendering of which Dreiser was praised, is a city he had never visited. This suggests the ability to seize upon essentials rather than accidentals in his milieu. The chief essential in the formation of this novel is what it was in *Sister Carrie*: Dreiser's thorough grounding in the nature of poverty. The book opens with a reminiscence of the beginning of his own family's worst days, when his mother had to go looking for work at the Terre Haute House, and includes the details of the children's stealing coal. It would be repetitious to go through this documentation again beyond noting that the initial paragraph, which sets the tone for what is to follow, pictures Mrs. Gerhardt with "such a shadow of distress" upon her face "as only those who have looked sympathetically into the countenances of the distraught and helpless poor know anything about."

Mencken, who wrote the first of his many pieces about Dreiser in reviewing *Jennie Gerhardt* under the title, "A Novel of the First Rank," praised its structure for a unity that the deflection of the reader's interest from Carrie's story to Hurstwood's prevented *Sister Carrie* from having. But the quality of slow movement that we observed there is now revealed to be another recurrent feature of Dreiser's work. Jennie "drifts" because it is her nature to lie open and fallow before experience, to be yielding, not dominating. Lester Kane "drifts," not helplessly like Hurstwood, but because he will not be pushed to the decision that convention demands. One of the reasons why Dreiser's characters often take on a grave magnitude lies in their refusal to be hurried, a refusal on his part as well as theirs. His sense of time is far more a sense of its endless flux than of its minute gradations. This novel starts in 1880, when Jennie is eighteen. She is in her forties by the end, but Dreiser gives hardly any attention here to the altering particulars of the external scene. His interest is centered upon her deepening awareness of what life does to people. Some readers object that the movement of this novel is too slow, that there is not enough foreshortened progression, that the characters' thoughts revolve too often over and over in the same groove. But he is writing to no clear-cut single climax. He brings Lester, before his death, to a general acceptance of Spencerian evolution, though with a sense still of great uncertainty, knowing that "the individual doesn't count much," and that whatever his own endowments of brain and talent, he has been much favored by the "luck" of wealth. Jennie is even less capable of coming to any "fixed conclusion as to the meaning of life." She wonders, to the end, "Was it all blind chance, or was there some guiding intelligence—a God?" The last sentence of the narrative still follows her groping thoughts as to what lies ahead for her: "Days and days in endless reiteration, and then—?"

Dreiser often seems to posit his characters rather than to

develop them, but *Jennie Gerhardt* contains his most fully realized group. Father Gerhardt is one of his minor masterpieces. Mrs. Gerhardt and the other children are more slightly sketched, but old Gerhardt is a reincarnation of Dreiser's father—who had been dead now almost a decade —freed of personal irrelevancies. Part of this feeling depends on the alteration of details. He is a strict Lutheran rather than a Catholic. When he goes off to look for work in Youngstown, while the rest of the family is in Cleveland, Dreiser is far more aware of the father's drearily solitary existence than he was able to be at the time of his own father's wanderings. With the death of Mrs. Gerhardt, Dreiser re-enacts what he had felt about the breakup of his own home. But here again, undistracted by what had been his own condition at that time, he can comprehend the fullness of the father's suffering as he says: "They all leave me. All my life goes to pieces." Dreiser remarks that the old man had grown "morose and crotchety," and had become impossible for young people to live with. At this point we get a glimpse into the way Dreiser's imagination worked— not by invention, but by probing to the core of a given situation and by discovering there more potentialities than mere observation or memory afforded. In the midst of old Gerhardt's somber reflections comes a recognition of the difference between his set theories and the quality of life. He sees that his other children, who are getting on now by the standards of the world, are selfish and cold, that Jennie whom he had dismissed as "not good" is alone thoughtful of him. He is won back to her in part by his fondness for his small granddaughter. By the end of his life he and Jennie have grown very close, and it is he who is asking her for forgiveness.

The world of the Gerhardts is set off against that of Senator Brander and the Kanes—again the two separate halves of the American world as he had observed it. Very few pages are given to Brander, who is dead when the novel is hardly more than under way; but Dreiser may have been constructing him in part from his memories, since the senator helps get Jennie's brother Bass out of jail, as a Terre Haute politician had helped Paul. With the Kane family Dreiser struck out into different material, bringing into his fiction the interest in American economic development which was to absorb him in his next two novels. He regarded Lester's father as a good representative of a whole phase of our history. Archibald Kane had "amassed a tremendous fortune, not by grabbing and browbeating and unfair methods, but by seeing a big need and filling it." He had built his wealth out of· production, by making good wagons and carriages, and selling them at a good profit. Dreiser saw him as a bigger man—"more generous and forceful"—than either of his sons. Robert was a born businessman, with a "hard incisiveness" that fitted him for the newer finance capitalism, but with none of his father's simple humanity. Dreiser drew thus his contrast between two stages of our development.

Lester, who falls in love with Jennie after Brander's death, while she is working as a maid in the home of one of the Kanes' friends, is a type by which Dreiser was much attracted. He saw Lester as "the natural product" of the fierce and dazzling "materialized forces" of the age, a new American. "His was a naturally observing mind, Rabelaisian in its strength and tendencies, but confused by the multiplicity of things, the vastness of the panorama of life, the glitter of its details, the unsubstantial nature of its forms, the uncertainty of their justification. Born a Catholic, he was no longer a believer in the divine inspiration of Catholicism; raised a member of the social elect, he had ceased to accept the fetish that birth and station presuppose any innate superiority; brought up as the heir to a comfortable fortune and expected to marry in his own sphere, he was by no means sure that he wanted marriage on any terms. Of course the conjugal state was an inspiration. It was established. Yes, certainly. But what of it? The whole nation believed in it. True, but other nations believed in polygamy. There were other questions that bothered him—such questions as the belief in a single deity or ruler of the universe, and whether a republican, monarchical, or aristocratic form of government were best. In short, the whole body of things material, social, and spiritual had come under the knife of his mental surgery and been left but half-dissected. Life was not proved to him. Not a single idea of his, unless it were the need of being honest. In all other things he wavered, questioned, procrastinated, leaving to time and to the powers back of the universe the solution of the problems that vexed him. Yes, Lester Kane was the natural product of a combination of elements—religious, commercial, social—modified by that pervading atmosphere of liberty in our national life which is productive of almost uncounted freedom of thought and action. Thirty-six years of age, and apparently a man of vigorous, aggressive, and sound personality, he was, nevertheless an essentially animal-man, pleasantly veneered by education and environment. Like the hundreds of thousands of Irishmen who in his father's day had worked on the railroad tracks, dug in the mines, picked and shoveled in the ditches, and carried up bricks and mortar on the endless structures of a new land, he was strong, hairy, axiomatic, and witty."

The somewhat repetitious but cumulatively impressive effect of this description is typical of Dreiser's way of introducing us to his characters. Lester, with a freedom that he really does not know what to do with, lives his own version of the doctrine of self-reliance, indifferent to or defiant of conventionality, and determined only to maintain his personality intact. He is easily distanced in business by his brother, since he lacks the "ruthless, narrow-minded insistence" that it demands for success. He recognizes in Jennie a greater reality than he has encountered in the women of his family's sphere, and establishes a home for her in Chicago. But his sceptical cast of mind, which keeps him alive as his brother is not, will in the end be the quality that causes him to give in to what his family exacts, as the price of his retaining his inheritance. Without any settled convictions, he will delay and waver, finally realize that he cannot "fly in the face of society," and agree to marry Letty Pace Gerald. Incidentally, though Dreiser has imagined Lester so thoroughly, his conception of Letty breaks into a register beyond his scope, and we see her only as we might in the society columns, when Dreiser starts the couple on their honeymoon "bound for the land of the Mikado."

The chief problem for Dreiser's plot is that a character like Lester's will not engage in decisive actions. Although he has left Jennie, he still supports her. But there is no further role for him to play, other than to grow older and die when his kidneys and arteries are worn out. His mind will not ever be made up, though he will meet death with a stoical courage. He will know at the end that Jennie had meant more to him than anyone else.

Here, as was not the case in *Sister Carrie*, Dreiser's chief creation is his heroine. Lester says to her, "You're a big woman, in your way," and Dreiser creates this largeness. This is partly because we feel her physical attraction, as we do not feel Carrie's, even though Dreiser hardly has words for this beyond those of the Sunday supplement: "There was that about her which suggested the luxury of love." She is even less developed mentally than Carrie. She cannot write very well; Lester once finds, with a fond smile, a list of some words he had used with their meanings written out opposite. There is little psychological interest in the stream of her rudimentary thinking, and the case against her has been summed up by Oscar Cargill, in *Intellectual America*, in a contrast with George Moore's Esther Waters: "Esther has character and force—she lives for us; Jennie is so much dough. It was folly for Dreiser to study again the fallen servant-girl after Moore had done so good a job of it. . . . Dreiser did not really know Jennie."

The issues raised here are crucial to an appreciation of Dreiser. He had no thought that he was studying "the fallen servant-girl." He was not detached from or superior to his material. He was writing not only of what he knew best, but of what he loved most. This was why Jennie remained his favorite heroine. The essential quality in her which draws first Brander and then Lester to her is "a largeness of feeling not altogether squared with intellect." In his first description of her Dreiser is at pains to convey the quality of "dreaming wonder" in her approach to life, and as always in such passages he keeps falling into the language of his sentimental poetry. When Jennie looks at a sunset, "Her soul was already up there, and its elysian paths knew the lightness of her feet."

Yet, in spite of his many stock phrases, he does manage to suggest her harmony with nature, particularly in the chapter recounting her reaction to childbirth. It is in such passages that we come to the real meaning of naturalism in relation to Dreiser. He did not work according to any theory of the novel, or of the animality of human beings. But his mind became more and more absorbed in understanding the broad processes of nature, and in making his fiction correspond with them.

In dealing with Jennie's bearing of Brander's child, Dreiser knew that his material was such as "the morality of our day has agreed to taboo." He was determined to give the strongest counterstatement he could achieve to the view expressed by "conceived in iniquity and born in sin," since he held that there was "nothing unclean in nature itself." He bore this out through the "serene and unfaltering" sense of fulfillment that Jennie found in her child, despite all the harshness of her father and the ostracism of the world. "Vague thoughts of sympathy and divine love permeated her soul. . . . She felt that she would love this child, would be a good mother to it if life permitted. That was the problem—what would life permit?"

In contrast to the conventional conception of the naturalistic novelist, Dreiser keeps saying, "Nature is so beautiful." During his trip to Europe just after the publication of *Jennie Gerhardt*, he discovered in the Dutch painters of the seventeenth century the acme of what he had been trying to present through his heroine: "the most perfect expression of commonplace beauty that the world has yet seen." His so often inadequate language could not yield the equivalent of the placid earthiness of Frans Hals, whom he admired most. Yet, regarding his canvases, Dreiser felt that this kind of beauty "had finally come to mean *to me* all that *I* can really hope for in art."

After Jennie's warm satisfaction in her baby, Dreiser pursues the question of what life will permit her. A more skillful writer could have foreshortened the account without losing its essentials, but Dreiser, when asked once why he did not write more short stories, said "I need a large canvas." As he had presented the slow falling action of Hurstwood's decline, now he wanted to present a slow rising action, not of Jennie's fortunes, but of her growing stature in human dignity.

Jennie is made to feel her guilt, but she is not to be hardened or corrupted by the world's blind judgments. She has to puzzle out for herself the critical distinctions between appearance and reality. She cannot feel that Brander's death has robbed her motherhood of all its consecration. She is instinctively eager to sacrifice herself for those she loves. It is interesting to note that Dreiser retains such terms as "consecration" and "sacrifice" in his ethics based upon acceptance of the processes of nature. When she is drawn by Lester's insistent passion, there is nothing in her of "hard, brutal immorality," and she remains devoted to him thenceforth. It should be remarked that she first yields to him as the only way she can see of helping her family when her father's hands have been badly burned at work. Dreiser says, in one of his key reflections about her: "Virtue is that quality of generosity which offers itself willingly for another's service, and, being this, it is held by society to be nearly worthless."

Her development, though not complex, is the development of a significant deepening in understanding. There is always a basis of sadness to her thoughts, and she regards her life as a failure. She knows that she remains bad in the world's eyes, and yet she continually struggles towards her conception of the good: "Did anything matter except goodness—goodness of heart?" By the time Dreiser has her voice this question, he has so persuaded us that the undercurrent of her feelings "ran so still because it was so deep" that he is no longer risking sentimentality. He has come to the basic emotion that he relied upon in his mother.

Jennie foresees that Lester will leave her eventually, as another judgment of the world upon her, though the thought of it is "terrible" to her. What adds cumulative power, and what made the book especially impressive to Mencken, is this growing sense that life is fated. Lester voices this to Jennie: "All of us are more or less pawns. We're moved about like chessmen by circumstances over which we have no control." When he leaves her in this mood, Jennie—in the kind of image we have already found in *Sister Carrie* to be so central to Dreiser's vision—"was like a rudderless boat on an endless sea."

This is the strain Mencken had in mind when he declared that Dreiser did not really fit with any contemporary theories of realism or naturalism: "His aim is not merely to record, but to translate and understand; the thing he exposes is not the empty event and act, but the endless mystery out of which it springs." Mencken found the most apposite analogy in these lines from *Oedipus Rex:* "O ye deathward-going tribes of man, what do your lives mean except that they go to nothingness?"

It is significant that Dreiser himself likened Hardy to the Athenian dramatists, and thought of him as "a great Greek wandering in a modern and hence an alien world." Hardy's sense of inexorable fate came closest to his own, just as some of Hardy's portraits of women, particularly of Tess, may have served to strengthen his confidence in trying to bring out to the full what he discerned in a character like Jennie's.

In an interview at the time of the book's appearance, he stated that he "did not believe in progress, only change," and in that statement cut through the shallow doctrinaire faith of the day. His main interest in the final chapters of his novel had been to portray his heroine faced to the full by the inexplicability of existence, by what Mencken in his review called its "meaninglessness." It would not have occurred to Dreiser that Jennie's passive acceptance of her lot would cause her to be thought of as "so much dough." He saw something not less than heroic in her refusal to be crushed. The final sequence through which he takes her is of an almost unrelieved darkness. When Lester leaves her, she is "depressed to the point of despair." But another crisis lies not far ahead. Her daughter, now a schoolgirl, contracts typhoid and dies, and Jennie is even more alone. Dreiser does not stop her story at this point, however; he has her try to go on with the life in which she can see no clear way, and she adopts first one and then a second child as a substitute for what she has lost. Here is another instance in which Dreiser's structure would have been more incisive if he had not introduced such further details. But he could not see how "the large, truthful lines" could be foreshortened without losing the massiveness he wanted.

Floyd Dell in his review sensed that Dreiser was giving a new significance to tragedy. "Tragedy? The word is loosely used nowadays. It means—what? 'Pity and terror' are said to be the emotional effects which distinguish it. 'Sympathy and awe' would perhaps be a better rendering of the Greek idea. A tragedy is the representation of a defeat which brings out the inherent nobility of the defeated one. . . . And Mr. Dreiser's Jennie has an authentic nobility."

Dreiser aimed, above all else, at stirring his readers to compassion, and the scene with which he ends this book is one of the most affecting he ever wrote. When Lester is stricken and knows himself to be dying, he sends for Jennie—his wife is on her way back from Europe—and they have a moment of reunion. But at the funeral Jennie must sit veiled and unrecognized at the rear of the church; and when she follows at a distance the procession to the station (Lester is to be buried at his birthplace in Cincinnati) Dreiser gives us one of his most powerful images of the excluded outsider. Jennie cannot go with the others onto the train, but must stand peering through the iron grating for a glimpse of the coffin, behind the last of the barriers "which divided her eternally from her beloved." This scene of awe is punctuated by exactly the right words of unconscious brutality from the baggageman: "Hey, Jack! Give us a hand here. There's a stiff outside!"

If heroism is the capacity to endure, Jennie possesses it. These final chapters are as sustained gravely level writing as any Dreiser ever did. Huneker called the book "eloquent in its humanity," and this kind of eloquence is strongest at its close. This is a further instance of the first thing we noted about Dreiser's prose—its deep grounding, at its best, in the rhythm of his emotions. As he recalled, among his first impressions of Chicago: "There was rhythm, rhythm, rhythm—and somehow men and crowds and every moving thing fell into it, although they were unconscious of it. And in the rain and under umbrellas or raincoats or covered wagon-tops, all life seemed to flow so softly and so smoothly. But to where? And for what?" This same sense of the endless flux and its inexplicability, greatly deepened by the generous resources of Jennie's nature, was what he brought to fullest expression in his second novel.

The Business Novel

LOOKING back to the years just after the appearance of *Jennie Gerhardt*, Dreiser could feel that this was the time when he had finally "risen against the wind." Led by the reviews of Mencken, Huneker, and Dell, *Jennie Gerhardt* was successful as *Sister. Carrie* had not been, though some commentators took the grudging position that "Times have changed, literary standards have lowered." In England his reputation had been quietly growing for some time. When Arnold Bennett visited this country in 1911, he told surprised interviewers that "Dreiser is the most significant figure among your writers," and was himself surprised to find how few of them had yet read *Sister Carrie* and how frequently people seemed to feel that they could dismiss its author merely by saying that he was "very crude."

It was to be characteristic of his working habits for the rest of his life for Dreiser to be engaged on several projects at once. He wrote Mencken shortly after he had finished *Jennie Gerhardt*, "I am going to do three more books," and added with the crudity which he never left behind him, "then if there is no money in the game I ['m] going to run a weekly. I can write a book every six months,

I think, so I won't be long out of the editing game unless perchance I should make a living this way. Who knows?" He had begun *The "Genius"* and was already well along with a first draft when Harper expressed much greater interest in the idea he had for a study of the businessman. He was writing out of so much stored-up energy at this time that he had also drafted over half of *The Financier* by the time *Jennie Gerhardt* appeared. He was planning his business novel as a trilogy, and when Grant Richards—the English publisher who had been following his work for some time —suggested that he take a trip to Europe and do a travel book in addition, Dreiser agreed, partly for the reason that Charles T. Yerkes, the businessman who was the prototype for his hero, had finished his career in London, and Dreiser could obtain there at first hand some of the material he needed.

He sailed at the end of November, spent the winter in England and on the Continent, and returned in the spring, just missing passage on the *Titanic*. He first amused but eventually disgusted Richards by being such a "worrying" traveler, so unable to relax and so continually anxious about his future. When Dreiser said, "I acknowledge the Furies, I believe in them, I have heard the disastrous beating of their wings," Richards could hardly realize how deeply this remark was rooted in Dreiser's past insecurity. Whether or not Dreiser learned much that he needed about Yerkes in London, ancient and Renaissance Italy afforded him several analogies for the predatory but magnetic quality that he saw in the American businessman. He studied the Medicis, he was so fascinated by the power of the Borgias that he set down a compressed history of them in the middle of one of his travel chapters, and he recaptured also some basic likenesses between imperial Rome and modern America.

Before writing up his travel impressions, he set himself to completing *The Financier*, and it was out in the fall of 1912. *A Traveler at Forty* is as a whole both superficial and ponderous, with its best passages those in which Dreiser conveys some of his wonder at so many things that were new to him, and its worst those which were akin to the "heavy gaiety" that he found in Berlin night life. But his new novel marked a departure in his fiction, and his arrival at the second of the two main types in which he worked. Here he was no longer drawing upon what he had learned primarily through his family: he was evolving a particular kind of documentary novel. In writing *Sister Carrie* he had had a sense of the historical significance of some of his material, but now he was shaping an account of the main drift of American economic development from before the Civil War. His sources were public, for the most part what he could read in the newspapers. He still seems to have kept no notebook, but to have soaked himself in his material until he was saturated with it. When it came to public documents and court records, he sometimes copied them verbatim, as he was to do again in *An American Tragedy*.

As for why he selected Yerkes for his prototype, Dreiser later told Masters that he "had looked into the careers of twenty American capitalists and that Yerkes was the most interesting of them." The actual process may have been less deliberate, since Yerkes's buccaneering career was at its height during Dreiser's own Chicago days. He had recently read Thomas W. Lawson's *Frenzied Finance*, and admired Gustavus Myers's investigations into the way the great American fortunes had been amassed. He declared that "the drift of the nation to monopoly and so to oligarchy" had begun to be apparent to him from his first exposure to Chicago—which sounds as though he were reading his later knowledge back into that time.

In any case his emphasis upon the facts he had observed was significantly different from the emphasis of the muckrakers. He made most explicit the attitude out of which *The Financier* was written in a passage in *A Hoosier Holiday* recalling his mood as he had moved east in 1894: "The spirit of America at that time was so remarkable. It was just entering on that vast, splendid, most lawless and most savage period in which the great financiers, now nearly all dead, were plotting and conniving the enslavement of the people and belaboring each other for power. These crude and parvenu dynasties which now sit enthroned in our democracy, threatening its very life with their pretensions and assumptions, were just in the beginning. John D. Rockefeller was still in Cleveland. Flagler, William Rockefeller, H. H. Rogers were still comparatively young and secret agents. Carnegie was still in Pittsburgh—an iron master—and of all his brood of powerful children only Frick had appeared. William H. Vanderbilt and Jay Gould had only recently died. . . . Giants were plotting, fighting, dreaming on every hand, and in this city [Buffalo], as in every other American city I then visited, there was a singing, illusioned spirit. Actually, the average American then believed that the possession of money would certainly solve all his earthly ills. You could see it in the faces of the people, in their step and manner. Power, power, power—everyone was seeking power in the land of the free and the home of the brave."

"And I," he added, "was dreaming of love and power, too." So much attraction to what he also disapproves is very different from the incisive critical judgment of Myers or the heartfelt denunciations of Upton Sinclair. Dreiser's mixed attitude had a good deal to do with his choice of Yerkes rather than one of the more typical robber barons. As Matthew Josephson summed up his findings on the leading embodiments of the type, a rank above Yerkes in wealth: "In general, they were puritanical and pious. Only one of them, Fisk, was given to free living, drinking, and flesh pots. . . . In private life they were generally discreet, sober, well-controlled, their strongest lust being the pecuniary appetite. The poverty which darkened the childhood of all of them save Morgan, son of a banker, lent them sobriety, and the Protestant teaching they received disciplined their will. . . . Not only did they have, as Veblen has said, Old Testament traits of ferocity, jealousy, clannishness and disingenuousness, but also the 'economic virtues' which are associated with Christian sobriety."

Yerkes, as Dreiser saw him, had none of "the bookkeeper's soul" that was attributed to Rockefeller. He loved not only wealth and power, but also women. But he was very different from Jim Fisk. He was not a roisterer, and he also loved art. His collection was not acquired wholesale, as was the case with many, but was a reflection of his own taste. In fine, when Dreiser told reporters that his aim was to portray his financier "unidealized and uncursed," he had in mind his most completely developed conception of a protagonist—one who could fuse, more effectively than anything else he had written so far, what Balzac and Spencer had helped teach him.

Cowperwood is no mechanical copy of Yerkes. He is

Dreiser's amplest expression of what he understood of the time-spirit, his contribution to the myth of the American hero. It will be illuminating, therefore, to separate the various strains that enter into his make-up, and particularly to note why he seems to live, as the more simplified business-man villains in the muckrakers' novels do not.

In a summary of his feelings for Paul, Dreiser said: "He was full of simple middle-class romance, middle-class humor, middle-class tenderness, and middle-class grossness—all of which I am very free to say I admire. After all, we cannot all be artists, statesmen, generals, thieves, or financiers." This reveals, to a greater degree than Dreiser was probably conscious of, the diverse elements of life that attracted him most profoundly. There were those relaxed qualities of Paul's with which he felt easily at home, and at the other extreme was the quality that he seems to have felt as a common denominator in his strangely miscellaneous list—the quality of power beyond good and evil. To his eyes a lawless character like Cowperwood, whose motto was "I satisfy myself," shared in the nature of the thief and of the artist as well as of the financier. In the opening pages, in which he portrayed his hero as a small boy watching in a tank at the fish market a lobster slowly but inevitably destroying a squid, Dreiser gave Cowperwood an image "which stayed with him all his life and cleared things up considerably intellectually."

The mature Cowperwood is no reader, but though he does not formulate his career in these terms, he is Dreiser's version of "the survival of the fittest," intermingled with traits of Nietzsche's "Superman," and possessing also what Dreiser calls a "Machiavellian" brain. In portraying Jennie, Dreiser had dwelt on the beauty in natural processes, but here he was impelled also to acknowledge their brutality. When asked, after publishing this novel, whether "the American financial type . . . so abundant and powerful, had ethically the right to be as it was or do as it was doing," his answer was that "in spite of all the so-called laws and prophets, there is apparently in Nature no such thing as the right to do or the right not to do, if you reach the place where the significance of the social chain in which you find yourself is not satisfactory." He added, with the same kind of expansiveness with which Whitman had attempted to cope with his America as it existed beyond the conventional formulas: "For my own part I am convinced that so-called vice and crime and destruction and so-called evil are as fully a part of the universal creative process as the so-called virtues, and do as much good." This does not mean that in other moods Dreiser was not shocked and shattered by what he saw, "chilled and stupefied by the way strength survives and weakness goes under." But the chief value of his fiction lies in the unflinching strength with which he recorded not the professed but the actual forces of his time. In the case of Cowperwood in particular Dreiser had an added source for creating his vitality, in that Cowperwood was the embodiment of so much that he himself had longed for and missed.

But the most elementary factor in accounting for this hero's continued appeal to readers should not be ignored. He is a version of the American success story, no matter how refracted from the official versions Dreiser had had to record for Marden in his early interviews with financiers. Indeed, at times a bare Horatio Alger pattern shows oddly through, as when Dreiser describes Cowperwood in his first job: "The books of Messrs. Waterman & Co., though fairly complicated, were child's play to Frank." To be sure, Dreiser's final intention was to carry Cowperwood as far as he could from the standard simplified fable. In an interview he gave just before *The Titan* was published, he dwelt at length on the mythical proportions he saw in his hero: "I doubt often whether the world is ever willing or even inclined to face its darker phases any more than it is capable of either experiencing or acknowledging its more exquisite pleasures. The capacity for life varies with individuals. In the main the vast majority are comparable to spindling undergrowth or grass. Here and there in this jungle which the will to live has produced are giant trees, sequoias, banyans."

Then, shifting his image, he spoke in the terms of his understanding of social Darwinism: "Giants seem to be preparing the earth for the average man, making it possible for billions to live in simple, oyster-like security, where, in a more brilliant or capricious state, only a few might survive." Here Dreiser was reaching the formulation that he was to articulate a few years later in an essay on "The American Financier": "Finally one is led to conclude that, by and large, the financial type is the coldest, the most selfish, and the most useful of all living phenomena. Plainly it is a highly specialized machine for the accomplishment of some end which Nature has in view. Often humorless, shark-like, avid, yet among the greatest constructive forces imaginable; absolutely opposed to democracy in practice, yet as useful an implement for its accomplishment as for autocracy."

When Dreiser published this, shortly after the First World War, he acknowledged his debt for many of his facts to Myers. But at the time when he conceived of his

Titan, his imagination was compelled far more warmly, and he ended the account of his intention by pointing out the most universal elements in his theme: "Some tales are too great to be told, or they need retelling. Certain I am of one thing, the age that produced at once the mechanical perfection of the world and its most colossal fortunes is classic. From that period certainly some Croesus, Lepidus or Maecenas is sure to show forth in fable, song, or story. In my limited search and with my selective tendencies none seemed of so great import, socially, sociologically, financially, philosophically as the individual whom I have selected. A rebellious Lucifer this, glorious in his somber conception of the value of power. A night-black pool his world will seem to some, played over by fulgurous gleams of his own individualistic and truly titanic mind. To the illuminate it will have a very different meaning, I am sure, a clear suggestion of the inscrutable forces of life, as they shift and play—marring what they do not glorify—pagan, fortuitous, inalienably artistic."

Clearly Dreiser envisaged as great heroic stature in Cowperwood as Marlowe did in Tamburlaine or Melville in Ahab. But Dreiser's method here was that of the historical novel, and he proceeded to involve his hero not only with the dominant forces of his time, but also with its detailed surfaces. Huneker, who came from Philadelphia, praised him for the authenticity of his picture of that city. Dreiser may have remembered what he needed from his desolate months there a decade before; but he pinned down Yerkes's operations by going through the files of the *Public Ledger,* and he also read local history.

Cowperwood is not poor. His father, a bank clerk at the time of his son's birth in the mid-eighteen-thirties, is on his way to a moderate and conservative success. He is sure that Andrew Jackson "was all wrong in his opposition to Nicholas Biddle." Yerkes came from Quaker stock, but Dreiser changed this to Episcopalian, and then in his revised edition of 1927 dropped the mention of any denomination, though he left the Cowperwoods with general religious respectability. He is very explicit that life had given his hero "no severe shocks nor rude awakenings," that "he had not been compelled to suffer illness or pain or deprivation of any kind." To be sure, he introduced as a motto to his opening chapter a quotation from *Richard III*: "I came into the world feet first and was born with teeth. The nurse did prophesy that I should snarl and bite." But he also dropped this in his revision, for though it suggested Cowperwood's kinship with Machiavelli, it was quite out of accord with the genial, cheerful, handsome young man ·whom he portrayed as having "nothing savage in his attitude, no rage against fate, no dark fear of failure." At the base of Cowperwood's character, as Dreiser saw it, there is no motivation out of grievance or frustration, but rather an instinctive, unimpeded response to the expanding possibilities of the age.

Indeed, he pronounces Cowperwood "a financier by instinct" from the first time he watches with intense curiosity his father counting money at his teller's window. His will to success and power develops early. At sixteen he is pressing his father, whom he now regards as much too cautious, to allow him to stop school and go to work. His first job is as a bookkeeper, but he knows that he will not do this kind of work long. He moves on to an investment house, but quickly comes to see that here he is "nothing more than a gambler's agent," that the real powers—the organizers and builders—are behind and beyond these scenes. In 1857, the year of the panic, he receives a twenty-five-thousand-dollar legacy from an uncle, and can begin to look ahead to the time when he will be in business for himself.

Cowperwood's reflections on the impending war enable Dreiser to picture his early hard maturity, and to present him also as an historical symbol. "The negro isn't worth all this excitement," he says, "but they'll go on agitating for him—emotional people always do. . . . It's hurting our Southern trade." When the war breaks out, he hopes that the North will win, but his behavior corresponds to that of Gould and Fisk. "He did not care to fight. That seemed silly for the individual man to do. Others might—there were many poor, thin-minded, half-baked creatures who would put themselves up to be shot; but they were only fit to be commanded or shot down. As for him, his life was sacred to himself and his family and his personal interests."

As the endless battles move to their conclusion, he speculates further: "He was not at all sure, for instance, that the negroes could be made into anything much more significant than they were. . . . He had no particular quarrel with the theory that they should be free—but beyond that he could not see that there was any great ethical basis for the contentions of their sponsors. The vast majority of men and women, as he could see, were not essentially above slavery, even when they had all the guarantees of a constitution formulated to prevent it."

Such passages contain the heart of Dreiser's interpretation of what happened to America as a result of the new careers open to the talents of the plutocrat. In Cowperwood's progress the Civil War was most significant in that it gave him his first great financial opportunity, that of making a loan to the government, as Jay Cooke and Francis M. Drexel had done.

By now Cowperwood is before us in his essential nature. Dreiser's intention is not to have him strike the reader as merely ruthless and cold. He *is* both, of course, but he is also capable of radiating great magnetism which Dreiser evokes especially in several passages dwelling on his gray-blue eyes: "Wonderful eyes, soft and spring like at times, glowing with a rich, human understanding which on the instance could harden and flash lightning. Deceptive eyes, unreadable, but alluring alike to men and women in all walks and conditions of life."

Dreiser sees him not only as an egotist, but as also possessing the mind of a creative artist in his own medium. Analogies with the Renaissance merchant prince—which will be more in keeping at the height of Cowperwood's career in *The Titan*—are first suggested when his architect introduces into the design for the door of his new office "a money changer's sign used in old Venice"; and the analogies begin to be developed by his growing fondness for the "magnificence" of paintings and tapestry.

His marriage was socially correct, made before he had really found himself, with a widow a few years his senior. Its quality can be summarized in the cool way Cowperwood looks ahead to having a son: "He liked it, the idea of self-duplication. It was almost acquisitive, this thought." Yerkes had six children by his first marriage, but the son and daughter Cowperwood begets are left very shadowy, far from the living center of his interests. The chief means by which Dreiser brings him to flesh-and-blood life is through the strength of his passion for his mistress, Aileen

Butler, the daughter of a Philadelphia Irish political boss. In her company Dreiser shows him no longer "defiant of life," but "courteous to it."

The chief dramatic development of the novel rises out of the contacts with local politics which Cowperwood established in the course of his loans. He finds the city treasurer compliant, and launches upon a course of speculating with the funds, to which the only limit seems to be the extent of his daring. His one rule for himself is "Never fail, never get caught." But the great Chicago fire creates a panic in the stock market, and the bosses make him a scapegoat; by now Aileen's father has found out about Cowperwood's relations with her, and has turned violently against him. But even when brought to trial Cowperwood remains unruffled, and Dreiser gives us another revealing summary of his state of mind: "He was strong, and he knew it, and somehow he always believed in his star. . . . Life was a dark, insoluble mystery, but . . . strength would win—weakness lose."

This Napoleonic strain sustains him even in prison, where he watches the night sky with the kind of absorption that will make it natural for him in his later career to contribute the money for the University of Chicago's observatory. For a while, as he thinks of the earth "floating like a little ball in immeasurable reaches of ether," his own life appears very trivial. But this mood is only fleeting, for he is "possessed with a sense of grandeur, largely in relation to himself and his affairs."

Cowperwood is certainly Dreiser's most confident accepter of change. He shakes off his depression over his temporary degradation, and even the prison attendants see a man "whose face blazed energy and power"—as Dreiser uses again his favorite active verb. A commuted sentence lets him out in time to take immediate advantage of the failure of Jay Cooke, which precipitated the panic of 1873, by selling short on everything and emerging once more a millionaire, with the resolution to turn to the West for a new career.

What saves Cowperwood's undaunted and almost imperturbable nature from being as unreal as that of an Alger hero is the scenes with Aileen, the most full-bodied love passages that Dreiser ever wrote. Aileen's character is far more coherently realized than Carrie's, and of a bold vitality that was no part of Dreiser's intention in portraying Jennie. There is luxuriance in her red-gold hair, an inclination to gorgeousness in her clothes, which again Dreiser describes with loving detail, as he does the period-piece rooms in which she and Cowperwood secretly meet. Breaking away from her convent-school training—a variation on what by now is a standard theme of Dreiser's—she brings a delight in anarchic freedom to match Cowperwood's. But the relation of their wills is defined in the remark that "she was drawn as planets are drawn to their sun." What makes Aileen poignant is that she is caught up beyond her control, as Cowperwood is not. In another of Dreiser's rare but effective uses of foreshadowing, she breaks out: "If you ever desert me, I'll go to hell. You'll see." When he is in prison, it is she who suffers more.

The single most effective stroke of creation in this book is Aileen's father. In him Dreiser's imagination was working most freely. Yerkes's mistress had been an actress, and Dreiser's way of involving Cowperwood's love affair with his political connections is his own. A St. Louis machine boss whom Dreiser had interviewed while he was a reporter there was named Edward Butler, but Dreiser seems to have blended into his character his accruing impressions of many other Irishmen. He had a particular flair for catching their qualities, as witness his portraits of Muldoon and Burke. But Butler is very different from either of these, as slow-paced and deliberate as Burke was quick and excitable. When you start reading any of the old politician's conversation, it sounds like that of the stage Irishman; but you gradually realize that though Dreiser's words are not exact, his tune is. He has fitted the rhythm of Butler's manner and gestures to the rhythm of his speech.

He has also produced his most powerful figure of a father. Dreiser documents Butler's background briefly through his rise from garbage collector to wealthy contractor and finally to political boss. He is solidly at ease when Cowperwood first goes to meet him in his house with its curtains of lace and its chairs of substantial red plush. He is humorous and warm-hearted as well as solemn and slow, and overpoweringly devoted to his daughter. His implacable anger will be in proportion. But when he confronts Aileen with her conduct, he is appalled to find in her a fighting will that equals his own. Dreiser has evolved in him a massive tragic helplessness, his agony matched to his wrath. As Dreiser foresees the scene of exposure of daughter by father, he reflects characteristically: "No good ever comes of violence."

He did not here present Cowperwood with any finality. He devised a frame for his novel within the context of his understanding of Darwinian science. He balanced the struggle to the death between the lobster and the squid, which gave young Cowperwood his initial glimpse of the laws of survival, with another passage of natural history at the close. He introduced this, after taking leave of Cowperwood on the train to Chicago with Aileen, whom he will now marry as soon as his divorce is granted. Here Dreiser's speculations took the form of a brief illustrative parallel with the character of the black grouper fish, which lives long "because of its very remarkable ability to adapt itself to conditions." It possesses a special power of altering its appearance, and thus, by simulating the color of things with which it has nothing in common, it strikes forth to get its living by subtle trickery. Dreiser regards the black grouper as representative "of the constructive genius of nature, which is not beatific." With this way of dismissing any conception of a beneficent divine will as merely delusive, he reflects, as though upon the victims of a Cowperwood: "Man himself is busy digging the pit and fashioning the snare, but he will not believe it. His feet are in the trap of circumstance; his eyes are on an illusion."

Dreiser had thought in this elementary way of the correspondences between men and animals in "A Lesson from the Aquarium," an essay he wrote during his first months of working for Street & Smith, comparing human behavior to that of small fish and sharks. A similar elementary strain of animal imagery runs through *The Financier*. Cowperwood in his first business venture is "like a young hound on the scent of game." He and Aileen "ran together temperamentally . . . like two leopards." Men on the stock exchange are "like a lot of gulls or stormy petrels, hanging on the lee of the wind, hungry and anxious to snap up any unwary fish." Such similes are very numerous, though they are not built into a consistent recurrent pattern as they would be by a writer more conscious of his resources. One most representative of Dreiser's vision occurs at Cowperwood's great moment of come-back in the panic: "Like a wolf prowling under glittering, bitter stars in the night, he was looking down into the humble folds of simple men and seeing what their ignorance and their unsophistication would cost them."

But Dreiser did not end *The Financier* with a picture of the triumph of grim natural force. Other reflections on chance and fate have been running through the book, if only as a subdued undertone. He says explicitly that Cowperwood had felt that "there was nothing to the Greek theory of being pursued by the furies." But when the bosses close in upon him to save themselves, it seemed as though "an untoward fate . . . was pursuing him." However, his view of life can give no countenance to such thoughts, and he pushes them aside. Dreiser appears to be suggesting in this way not merely that Cowperwood is undauntedly self-reliant, but also that there is a limitation in his vision. In a final passage after the reflections on the black grouper, and as a second departure from the realistic theory of fiction that everything should be contained within the narrative itself, Dreiser borrows the standard device of prophecy, with an equally standard allusion to the witches in *Macbeth*. What is promised for Cowperwood is "a world of mansions, carriages, jewels, beauty; a vast metropolis outraged by the power of one man; a great State seething with indignation over a force it could not control; vast halls of priceless pictures; a palace unrivaled for its magnificence; a whole world reading with wonder, at times, of a given name." But there will also be great sorrow, and the final cryptic destiny held out for this hero is "Master and no master, prince of a world of dreams whose reality was disillusion."

The further expansion of Cowperwood's powers, rather than any final judgment upon him, is the main tenor of *The Titan*, the second part of what Dreiser had now subtitled "A Trilogy of Desire." Opinions divided sharply over the relative success of these first two parts. Mencken wrote Dreiser about *The Financier*: "No better picture of a political-financial camorra has ever been done. It is wholly accurate and wholly American." But by the time of his printed comment Mencken, having changed his mind somewhat, criticized for the first time Dreiser's weight of detail as slowing down his story too much. He made no such reservations about *The Titan*: "It is the best thing you have ever done, with the possible exception of *Jennie Gerhardt*. . . . It is the best picture of an immoralist in all modern literature."

Masters took the opposite view. He said of *The Financier*: "It is a big thing, and shows a big grasp of things. I believe no American writer understands the facts of modern American life as you do. And your 'sceptical daring' is immense. . . . If you ever get a theme which focuses all your powers and which comes forth fused and molten, you will add that illumination to your work which makes art." But he did not find this fusion in *The Titan*: "You will do infinitely better work than this. This is not satisfying. There's the power there, and the giant massing of details—but somehow you have not nursed or caressed, lived with and reproduced the spirit of the thing. . . . Now you loved Jennie, and you made everyone love, so understand her. Of course no one could love Cowperwood, but you don't make us hate him, or even greatly dread him."

Dreiser had begun to be intimate with Masters when he

went to Chicago in the early winter of 1913 to complete his knowledge of Yerkes's dealings there. In talks with reporters he revealed the extent to which he had himself been caught up into Cowperwood's mood. He objected that the wild spirit that had created the earlier Chicago was now dead—"the wilder the better for those who are strong enough to survive." During his weeks there he was greatly attracted by a young actress at the new Little Theater, who was a friend of Dell's, and he utilized the episode (very slightly altered) as Cowperwood's affair with Stephanie Platow. To this degree he had become identified in his own imagination with his conquering hero.

Dreiser's main structural problem in *The Titan* was how to continue to heighten Cowperwood's stature. A man of force when he laid siege to Chicago, he was to rise to far greater power than any he had enjoyed in Philadelphia. Dreiser endeavored to keep pace with this advance by a series of analogies to match its stages. On his arrival Cowperwood knows that he is regarded as an ex-convict, "an Ishmael." But he determines to conduct his fortune so that he can "present himself, like a Hamilcar Barca in the heart of Spain or a Hannibal at the gates of Rome, with a demand for surrender and a division of spoils." As he sweeps everything before his will he strikes men as "either devil or prince, or both." To one of the young actresses who has been reading Marlowe and Jonson, he is "a great personage of the Elizabethan order." Dreiser has many other epithets to fit his rise. When Cowperwood has gained his monopoly of the street railways and has built the Loop, he towers over the city, "a colossus." Passing on to bend the laws of the state to his own ends, he is seen variously as "a superman," "a half-god or demi-gorgon," as he holds fast to his attitude "of Promethean defiance, which had never yet brooked defeat."

But it is one thing for Dreiser to envisage Cowperwood, and quite another for him to enable the reader to respond to his hero in anything like these dimensions. Dreiser had a much bigger subject here than in *The Financier*, a broad canvas that his knowledge of Chicago might have let him fill with its crowded figures. But he was faced with the problem of dramatizing the details of more complicated finance. He can present Cowperwood's feeling for the streetcar lines ("the tinkle of car-bells . . . was in his blood"); but when Cowperwood-Yerkes advances into the area of securing franchises, piling one corporation on another, and engaging in the then newly developed art of manipulating holding companies, the material tends to become too abstract to handle.

In the presentation of Cowperwood's gallery of women there is another and even more crucial weakness in what Dreiser would have regarded as one of his greatest strengths. No woman can hold Cowperwood long, but Dreiser had no skill in differentiating between the women, and they become merely a series of stereotypes for Cowperwood's needs. Here Stuart Sherman was right in his objection that the structure of this novel is "a sort of huge club-sandwich, composed of slices of business alternating with erotic episodes." And unfortunately Dreiser's worst failure is with the girl upon whom Cowperwood stakes most—Berenice Fleming, the "dream girl" of eighteen who is meant to be the most exquisite being he has ever met. But though Dreiser attributes varied intellectual and artistic qualities to her—gifts for dancing and painting and writing —he never apprehends any of these concretely enough to let us believe in them. There is a sentimental vulgarity in her whole conception, wholly different from the warm coarseness of Aileen.

Aileen continues to be an emotional center of the book as she finds herself excluded from Chicago society and realizes that she is losing Cowperwood through the reckless impulsiveness that had first attracted him. As Dreiser notes, she is not "hard enough to succeed." And as she begins to drink and to try to distract herself with other men while still caring only for Cowperwood, there is a reality in her suffering which Dreiser seems not to have suspected to be lacking in all her successors.

This is the most serious instance in any of his books so far of the sharp boundaries of his range. He can understand the outsider, but he can usually only glamorize the insider —or what in the realm of women and art an outlaw like Cowperwood, who has driven his way up to the top, would continue to possess. There is a comparable insecurity in his handling of Cowperwood's art collection. Dreiser, absorbed in recounting its growing splendor, speaks in equal terms of its Rembrandts and its Bouguereaus; he was never much more discriminating about it than when he described Cowperwood's first trip to Europe: "Here and there was an artist, such as Lord Leighton, Dante Gabriel Rossetti, or Whistler, to whom he was introduced." That "such as" tells the story. Cowperwood-Yerkes, to be sure, may have been as undiscriminating as this, but Dreiser indicates no awareness of any flaws in his taste.

The structure of *The Titan* is static, as that of *The Financier* is not, despite all the business and political struggles through which Cowperwood passes. This is owing partly to the greater suitability for Dreiser's slow imagination of one central dramatic situation instead of a whole series. Cowperwood's defiant meetings with the older lords of the city (who are based on Armour, Field, and the rest) and the turbulent scenes in the city council when it finally revolts from his domination—these were the things in which Zola's plastic gifts for creating crowds of people in conflict would have been supreme, and where Dreiser is most lumbering.

But the chief reason why so much action is not more dynamic is that Dreiser's desire to exalt his hero has in a sense raised him above the level of being affected by victory or defeat. Conceiving Cowperwood as endowed with "beauty and resourcefulness" of mind, Dreiser cannot put him into a situation where his ruthless qualities will show him at real disadvantage. He never makes him as plain-spoken as Yerkes was in one of his most frequently quoted adages: "The secret of success in my business is to buy old junk, fix it up a little and unload it upon other fellows." Cowperwood's Olympian quality also robs his show-down with Governor Swanson (whose prototype was Altgeld) of some of its trenchancy. When Cowperwood, engaged in "fixing" the state legislature to extend his franchises, calls on the Governor in the hope of bribing him also, Swanson sees the issue between them: it is that between "greed, over-weening ambition, colossal self-interest," and all the ideals and hopes of a struggling democracy. But Cowperwood tries to cut across their differences in the way that makes him most fascinating to Dreiser, and declares: "The men who are fighting you are fighting me. I am a scoundrel because I am selfish and ambitious—a materialist. You are not a scoundrel, but a dangerous person because you are an idealist." When Swanson turns him down in this effort to make a common cause between them, Cowperwood is not at all vindictive. He does not play a vigorous part in hounding the Governor out of office by branding him a socialist and an anarchist, as a character imagined more completely within the actual forces of history would have done and as Yerkes actually did.

This naturally does not mean that Dreiser should have confined himself to what Yerkes or anyone else did. But he had envisaged in his hero more than he was able to bring out through any action he managed to involve him in. Cowperwood, like the action, is static, since he passes through every experience virtually untouched. He is a vigorous and shrewd animal who can be lessened only by a decline in physical vitality, beaten only by death. Yet Dreiser concluded this second part on the theme of a final judgment: "Rushing like a great comet to the zenith, his path a blazing trail, Cowperwood did for the hour illuminate the terrors and wonders of individuality. But for him also the eternal equation—the pathos of the discovery that even giants are but pygmies, and that an ultimate balance must be struck."

Some feeling on Dreiser's part that he had already given the essential portrait of his immoralist, and had little more to add, may have been what deflected him at this point from going ahead to complete the trilogy. He never, indeed, really dropped his idea for *The Stoic*; it kept cropping up in his correspondence. He worked on it sporadically in the early nineteen-twenties just before he settled to *An American Tragedy*, and when he was in Europe again in 1926 he gathered some more material about Yerkes. His recurrent interest in the theme also showed itself in the revision he then undertook of *The Financier*. The primary intention in this was to cut sixty thousand words out of a book running to over a quarter of a million. But he ended by doing far more than a paste-and-scissors job: he rewrote the whole novel, adding many passages as well. A detailed comparison of the two versions is beyond our scope here, but the very fact of the revision serves to remind us that Dreiser's manuscripts were never finished.

His whole attitude toward them was as far as possible from that of the self-conscious craftsman. Whenever possible he turned to friends for suggestions, as when he told Dell to be as free as he liked in pointing out necessary cuts in *The "Genius."* Later on he trusted his pages more and more to his various secretaries. He never grew beyond an oppressive sense of his uncertain "struggles and flounderings" with each new beginning. Furthermore, he took an unusually impersonal attitude toward what he had written, with hardly any of the customary possessive pride. He wanted his work to be as right as it could be made—if not by himself, then by another.

The revision of *The Financier* involved both gains and losses, though the effect of the whole is hardly more altered than Whitman's poems ordinarily were by the endless changes that struck his wavering fancy between the various editions of *Leaves of Grass*. A reader can barely notice much change of pace through the shortening of what still remains a very long book. Some unnecessary documentation is eliminated, but the elision of several passages of Cowperwood's reflections curtails our sharing in the evolution of his conscious attitudes. One passage just after Cowperwood learns that he is to be brought to trial would seem to be as significant a formulation as any in the book: "Whatever he was, he was neither a hypocrite nor a fool.

He did not delude himself concerning himself or others.
. . . He would have agreed with Machiavelli that, other
things being equal, fortune is always with him who plans.
He was no fatalist; or if he was, he would not give fate the
opportunity to say that he had not put up a good fight—
had not taken advantage of every single opportunity. He
was no coward; and, above all, he was no moralist suffering
from an uneducated conscience. He saw no morals anywhere—nothing but moods, emotions, needs, greeds. People talked and talked, but they acted according to their
necessities and desires, just as he did, only as a rule they
were not quick and clever as he was. For this, sometimes,
he was sorry for them. At other times he was not."

Again, for another instance, we are deprived of one of
Dreiser's own most characteristic meditations upon the
tragedy of life, rising out of the contrast between Cowperwood's undauntable self-reliance and the helplessness of his
accomplice the city treasurer: "The damnable scheme of
things . . . whereby whole masses suffer who have no
cause to suffer, and, on the other hand, whole masses joy
who have no cause to joy. . . . We suffer for our temperaments, which we did not make, and for our weaknesses
and lacks, which are no part of our willing or doing."

In regard to the additions, it is interesting to note that
they are far more frequent in the last half of the book,
suggesting that Dreiser got more caught up into his old
subject as he went along. He made several gains in concrete
presentation—of the room in which Cowperwood and
Aileen are tracked down by Pinkerton detectives and of
their reaction in that situation; of the role played by
wealthy Senator Simpson, who is now given explicitly the
appearance and manner of his Roman equivalent. But the

largest single addition is of very doubtful value—a dozen pages of the summarizing speeches of the lawyers at the trial. This is the kind of documentation of which Dreiser was to make so much in *An American Tragedy*, but there it is far more thoroughly integrated with the main theme of the novel.

Despite his reabsorption in the subject, Dreiser did not go on from this revision to *The Stoic*. In the early nineteen-thirties he was thinking of it again, though with his by then developed political beliefs he realized that his readers might regard it as "decidedly unsocial and even ridiculous coming from a man who wants social equity." Yet he resolved to write it "just that way." It was always to be deferred, however, until the last months of his life. Then out of a sense that he still had left something unsaid he brought the manuscript almost to a close, turning for advice to James T. Farrell and relying greatly upon his devoted second wife. At the time of his death all that was lacking was a final chapter which Mrs. Dreiser could put together from his notes.

The Stoic rounded out Cowperwood's career, as he moved on from Chicago to New York and then to England, where he developed the London Tube. The European portions in particular are lacking in the mass of intimately possessed details that made *The Titan* solid even when dull. Cowperwood, nearing sixty, is endowed with the same charm that Dreiser always felt in him: "ruddy, assured, genial, a gardenia in his lapel, gray hat, gray shoes, and swinging a cane." But what should have been the great final scene is largely missed. Estranged from Aileen, he dies in a New York hotel, and his body is brought by his servants into his Fifth Avenue mansion only by stealth. An overpowering image of insecurity might have been evoked as his lifeless form lies there through the night in the midst of these vast, lonely, and now meaningless rooms, which are soon to be stripped of their splendor as his overextended fortune crashes to nothing.

But Dreiser hardly dwells on this, and does not make it his climax, since his attention has been deflected by an episode that would have been no part of his original scheme. This is the conversion of Berenice, after Cowperwood's death, to the mysticism of *Bhagavad-Gita*. Dreiser seems to have thought that he could bring out in this way the necessity of losing the self in the larger not-self, if the ultimate blankness of Cowperwood's world was to be redeemed. But the heretofore petted and spoiled Berenice seems no more real as a convert than at the moment when, returning from her study of the sacred books of the East, she takes up her residence at the Plaza. She seems hopelessly tainted by the kind of specious religiosity that had seeped into Dreiser's consciousness during his years in California. Although he means us to view her sympathetically, her version of yoga is inescapably that of Hollywood.

Quite apart from this last episode the reasons for which we shall examine when we come to Dreiser's later thought —there is the question of his final judgment of his hero. Cowperwood remains unaltered to the end, his energies and appetites waning only a little until he falls a victim of Bright's disease. Visiting the spot where Thomas à Becket was murdered, he asks: "Was any man noble? . . . He was scarcely prepared to believe it. Men killed to live—all of them—and wallowed in lust in order to reproduce themselves. In fact, wars, vanities, pretenses, cruelties, greeds, lusts, murder, spelled their true history, with only the weak running to a mythical saviour or god for aid. And the strong using this belief in a god to further the conquest of the weak. And by such temples or shrines as this. He looked, meditated, and was somehow touched with the futility of so much that was still so beautiful."

But the daily philosophy by which Cowperwood lives is what he reveals in an offhand remark to one of his business associates: "Neither of us can do much more than eat a little, drink a little, play about a little while longer, that's all." Despite the title he seems far more of an Epicurean than a Stoic—though even this only in the popular sense. His easy acceptance of change—the element Dreiser is always stressing in him—removes him from any tragic destiny. Masters was right: Cowperwood is not a figure whose death we can regard with much awe.

Yet when all the strictures have been considered, *The Financier* and some stretches of *The Titan* stand among Dreiser's powerful imaginative acts. What they added to our literature may be pointed up by a few more comparisons, in this case with the other business novels of the period in which Dreiser's trilogy was conceived. Most of those written in the spirit of the muckrakers' investigations —like David Graham Phillips's *The Master Rogue* (1905) —hardly do more than present their protagonists in thinly journalistic terms, with no penetration beneath the surface of their acts to their motivation in the forces of the time. Upton Sinclair in his two attempts in this genre, *The Metropolis* (1907) and *The Moneychangers* (1908), has none of the involvement with his material that made *The Jungle* so powerful. Here he is merely denouncing from a distance what he disapproved, but what his imagination has hardly begun to possess. At the opposite angle of approach is Edith

Wharton's *The Custom of the Country* (1913). This is not strictly a business novel since Mrs. Wharton, like Henry James, was aware of the gulf separating "downtown," the world of affairs, and "uptown," the world of society; and Undine Spragg, a girl from the Middle West in conquest of New York, remains her central figure. But as a means of dramatizing her contrast between the old New York and the new, Mrs. Wharton makes a conscientious study of Elmer Moffatt, a businessman from Undine's home town, who will end up a billionaire railroad king, and to whom Undine will finally revert. Mrs. Wharton, as the insider looking out, can endow him with a kind of "epic effrontery," but he never quite escapes being a mere grotesque.

Comparison with Norris's *The Pit* is on closer grounds, since Curtis Jadwin's efforts to corner the wheat take place in the Chicago stock market during Yerkes's period in the city. Dreiser's Chicago in *The Titan* is not realized with so much dense authenticity as it was in *Sister Carrie*. He invokes the vaster sphere of Cowperwood's operations as "this Burns of a city . . . with the grip of Caesar in its mind, the dramatic force of Euripides in its soul." But he does not have the gifts of folk poet or tragedian to make this rhetoric operative in his story. Nor, as we have seen, does he have Norris's gift for the sweeping panorama at the moment of panic. But Norris's scrutiny of his material is far less coherently serious than Dreiser's. *The Pit* is continually being deflected into a conventional love story of how Laura Jadwin kept her husband. Norris seems only intermittently concerned with what Dreiser never lets us forget, the manifold drives that are ever present in Cowperwood. Put another way one might say that Norris is rarely able here to imbed his characters as deeply in life as Dreiser manages to do. Unlike *McTeague,* there is nothing in *The Pit* so sustained as the running series of animal images in *The Titan,* of which this glimpse of Union Club members is representative: men "with eyes and jaws which varied from those of the tiger, lynx, and bear to those of the tolerant mastiff and the surly bulldog."

The best business novel of the decade preceding *The Financier* is Robert Herrick's *Memoirs of an American Citizen* (1905). Herrick, three years older than Dreiser, a native of New England who taught writing for many years at the University of Chicago, was intimately acquainted through his reading with both the literary and the social movements of the age that Dreiser approached more gropingly. Many of Herrick's long list of novels may not have enough creative vitality to carry them, but in *Memoirs* he gave his best expression to what he saw very steadily as the destructive forces in our society. He had understood these forces in more clear-cut terms than Dreiser was to do until much later. From the night that Van Harrington, an outcast young man from Indiana, arrives in Chicago in 1876 and has to sleep out on the waterfront, up to his induction into "the millionaires' club"—the Senate—following his support of the Spanish-American War, his rise is interwoven with the tendencies of the time that made it possible. Like Cowperwood he keeps asking himself, "What was there to live for except success?"—though unlike Cowperwood he is himself a reader of Darwin and Spencer while he forces his way up in the meat-packing business. Herrick may relate him somewhat too patly to events by having him be one of the jurors in the trial of the Haymarket anarchists and cast his cynical vote as the big men still above him expect him to. But a very effective contrast is drawn between the glimmer of the Fair and the poverty which cuts away from it, as it also does from the selfish heights which Harrington has now reached. In a way that Dreiser ignored, Herrick then goes on to study how such a character, checked by no scruples, will inevitably corrupt the men who work for him.

But the whole book is told with the hero as narrator: a poor device in a novel with Herrick's intention, since—in making Harrington so coolly conscious of the evil role he is playing—it serves to deprive him of some of Cowperwood's substance. The use of this device seems to mark the chief difference between Herrick and Dreiser, and to bring us out approximately where we were after contrasting the streetcar strikes in Howells and in Dreiser. Herrick's mind was clearer in its values than Dreiser's was, and—though he does not intrude on the narrative—he keeps judging Harrington at every step. The lack of final judgment on Dreiser's part made *The Titan* decline from *The Financier*, and *The Stoic* be hardly worth the trouble of finishing. But it also meant that in the genre of the business novel, where the oppositions tended to be seen in sharply limited patterns of black and white, Dreiser in the initial conception and handling of his hero broke through to something more impure and more dangerous—and more alive. Dorothy Dudley was especially astute in noting how much there was in Dreiser's nature that put him among "the immoral, indecorous, conquering Americans, allowed to live when they dealt in the medium of money, but apt to be censored when they worked with words." In writing about Cowperwood, therefore, he was curiously both outsider and insider.

To be sure, he gave a generalized description of "the Titans" as those "who without heart or soul, and without any understanding or sympathy with the condition of the rank and file, were setting forth to enchain and enslave them." But the reader never feels that Dreiser is wholly involved in this verdict. As a result he shared, as the mass of people of his time shared, in being attracted to what might well destroy, in a curiously blurred dream that combined Horatio Alger with Darwin and Nietzsche. One must also add that Dreiser's lack of final discrimination again defines his limitations sharply, as it keeps a Cowperwood far below an Ahab as a symbol of the terrifying reaches of the individual will.

The Genius Himself

THE "*GENIUS*" is Dreiser's poorest novel, the one least rewarding to reread. It had a very divided audience, even among his friends. Mencken hurled against it all the adjectives he could readily think of, most of which still stick: "flaccid, elephantine, doltish, coarse, dismal, flatulent, sophomoric, ignorant, unconvincing, wearisome." The basic difficulty was that here Dreiser was writing a novel too closely autobiographical to be viewed in any perspective. The common denominator in all his most living characters so far was, as we have seen, his deep personal involvement with them; yet this was counterbalanced by the fact that in no case had he been writing directly in his own person.

It is otherwise with Eugene Witla. Although he is a painter, whose work is modeled in part on that of Dreiser's friend Everett Shinn, he re-enacts all the main stages in Dreiser's career up to the writing of *Jennie Gerhardt*. He comes from the Middle West to New York, he marries Angela Blue, he goes through a nervous breakdown and regains his health by a job on the railroad, he is deflected from art into advertising and has a great success as art director and managing publisher of United Magazines until he loses this position and returns to his proper work. There are a few marked differences: Witla's first painting scores a great triumph (as *Sister Carrie* did not), his breakdown is brought on primarily by overwork, and Angela finally dies in childbirth. But these differences were not enough to enable Dreiser to detach himself from the material and to judge its proportions. He possessed none of the hard artistic control that such an act demands when the material is so completely the writer's memories. As a consequence *The "Genius"* does not have the full genuineness of his autobiographies, and is yet very formless as a *Bildungsroman*. As Mencken said, it is "as gross and shapeless as Brünnhilde."

It has, however, a secondary interest in filling out a little further the pattern of Dreiser's developing thought. Witla phrases again some of the first shattering effect of evolutionary theory upon him: "Nature seemed lavish of its types and utterly indifferent to the persistence of anything. He came to the conclusion that he was nothing, a mere shell, a sound, a leaf." In his worst depression he could not avoid the feeling that the chief characteristic of existence was "malevolence." But towards the end of the book Witla begins to speculate more widely. Dreiser has him quote a long passage from the English naturalist, Alfred Russel Wallace, who presupposes "some vast intelligence" guiding the universe. Then—in a way that may well have surprised Dreiser's readers at the time, but that prepares us for his later growing concern with the meaning of religion—Witla attempts to reconcile Wallace's thought with Christian Science. In his first draft of the manuscript, back in 1911, Dreiser had Witla now discover a beauty in the speculations which had formerly tortured him, and declare that "there is a ruling power" that "is not malicious." Indeed, he looks at a passage in Spencer's *First Principles* which had once impressed him deeply, and reflects that he has found "something better" in *Science and Health*.

But this first draft had come to a happy ending, with Witla marrying Suzanne, the girl over whom he had lost his job. Such an ending grew to seem false to Dreiser, and after his long immersion in the brute forces of Cowperwood's world he could hardly close on a note of calm sureness. And so Witla, whose affair with Suzanne had been permanently broken up by her mother, veers away from any religious acceptance, and Dreiser remarks that he was not much changed from what he had been, "only hardened intellectually and emotionally—tempered for life and work." In the last scene he is reading again the "astonishing chapters" on "the Unknowable," in which Spencer voices his awe at "the consciousness that without origin or cause, infinite space has ever existed and must ever exist." To this Witla adds: "That is certainly the sanest interpretation of the limitations of human thought I have ever read."

Dreiser himself commented on the quotation marks in the novel's title: "I haven't committed myself at all. I merely put it up to the public." In a way that the novelist did not realize, Witla seems impossible as an artist. One can just manage to be a writer by main force as Dreiser did, but one cannot be a painter without continual training in his craft. Native talent might have carried Witla to his first quick success, but it seems scarcely possible that, after his long deflection into being a businessman, he would again emerge so soon in full power. And the insecure knowledge and taste that was revealed in Dreiser's enumeration of Cowperwood's art collection here appears far more devastatingly. Once we have read of Witla's "ideal" studio—with its tapestries representing old Rhine castles, its eleven-branched candelabra, its bust of Nero, and its great wooden crucifix flickering in the shadows—we can hardly believe in him at all.

And yet, surprisingly, Dreiser had thought quite coherently about the kind of work he attributes to Witla. He knew and admired Sloan and Luks and Glackens, as well as Shinn, and he had seen in "the Ash-Can school," as it was scornfully dubbed by the critics, real bonds with his own aims. He makes us feel this in his many descriptions of Witla's canvases, which stress the deep importance for our culture of their native realism. Witla "loved the thought of making the commonplace dramatic," and his subjects indicate how avidly Dreiser had enjoyed the new school, as he had previously enjoyed the photographs of Stieglitz. Incidentally his real if untrained interest in painting is further substantiated by his mentioning to one of his later bibliographers that he had drafted, before he had published anything, a life of George Inness which, he said, was "a good thing which I wish I had." What attracted him to Inness comes out in *A Hoosier Holiday* when he mentions in passing how Indiana's hazy dreamful atmosphere might have been caught by such a painter. Inness's approach to his medium and material was very different from that of the Ash-Can school, but perfectly attuned, in Dreiser's view, to evoking the earlier American scene.

Witla's first great success is with "Six O'Clock," the hour of the workday's end—which, incidentally, had also been the title of one of Dreiser's magazine sketches. What Witla portrays is "a mass of East Side working girls flooding the streets. . . . There were dark walls of buildings, a flaring gas lamp or two, some yellow lighted shop windows, and many shaded half seen faces—bare suggestions of souls and pulsing life."

Witla also paints "Fifth Avenue in a Snow Storm," but a more characteristic subject is "Engines Entering a Freight Yard." We get a renewed impression of Dreiser's own accurate eye, and his fellow feeling with Witla's sense of beauty-in-ugliness in his evocation of this scene: "the smoke of the engines towering straight up like tall whitish-gray plumes, in the damp, cold air, the sky lowering with blackish-gray clouds, the red and yellow and blue cars standing out in the sodden darkness because of the water. You could feel the cold, wet drizzle, the soppy tracks, the weariness of 'throwing switches.' "

We also feel Dreiser's involvement in the debate among the critics, since it is *his* debate as well. The conventional judgment ridicules Witla's work and dismisses it, as it first dismissed Sloan and the rest of his group: "Broken window shutters, dirty pavements, half frozen ash cart drivers, overdrawn, heavily exaggerated figures of policemen, tenement harridans, beggars, panhandlers, sandwich men—of such is *Art* according to Eugene Witla." But one critic sees in these pictures what Dreiser most wanted in his writing: "A true sense of the pathetic . . . the ability to indict life with its own grossness, to charge it prophetically with its own meanness and cruelty in order that mayhap it may heal itself; the ability to see wherein is beauty—even in shame and pathos and degradation." The keenness with which Dreiser dramatizes the issues in his debate makes us realize how much he may have been strengthened in his own resolves by his awareness of such vital allies among the new painters.

The novel as a whole contains unquestionably some of Dreiser's worst writing. This resulted in part from his lack of detachment, and some of the scenes of tension with Angela read like stock melodrama as scenes often do that are loosely recollected rather than transformed. Dell sensed something like this when he wrote: "There is passage after passage, incidènt after incident, in which you have got everything but the soul of the action—something I have never known you before to miss." Dreiser had been writing at headlong speed—*The "Genius"* was finished only a few months after *The Titan*, in the summer of 1914—and one sign of this is his repeating over and over the same few descriptive words. Just as Cowperwood was called "trig" far too often, so is Witla "subtle" and "artistic." The worst banalities are in the language of love. These no doubt sounded natural to Dreiser's ears, as when Angela calls Witla "Honey-bun." Her pet name for her sister is "Babyette." "Say! that's a dandy pet name," says one of Witla's friends, the painter Smite. John Cowper Powys, who thought highly of *The "Genius,"* defended the way in which "people are permitted to say those things which they actually do say in real life—things that make you blush and howl, so soaked in banality and ineptitude are they." But any defense on such grounds soon breaks down; and it will not cover what are probably the most tasteless passages in all of Dreiser, those in which Witla addresses Suzanne: "Oh, Flower Face! Oh, Silver Feet! Oh, Myrtle Bloom!"

The chief thing we have to remind ourselves of in connection with *The "Genius"* is why it was an important book, not only for Powys but for Sherwood Anderson and Randolph Bourne. The situation in American literature was still substantially the same as it had been when Henry Adams noted that except for Whitman no American artist "had ever insisted on the power of sex, as every classic had always done." Bourne commented on the crippling effect of this in his review of *The "Genius,"* and added: "That Mr. Dreiser is our only novelist who tries to plumb far below this conventional superstructure is his great distinction. . . . His hero is really not Sister Carrie or the Titan or the Genius, but that desire within us that pounds in manifold guise against the iron walls of experience."

What had been present in all Dreiser's novels so far, but incidental to their main themes, engaged the center of his attention when he wrote *The "Genius"* in prolonged revolt against the doctrine of "one life, one love." He was determined to speak out, as he did again in his autobiographies, where he acknowledged sex as "the controlling and directing force that it is." When writing about Paul he said that he had never known anyone more interested in women "unless perchance it might be myself." On the theme that life is "incurably varietistic and pluralistic in its tastes and emotions," he went ahead to say that he had found it "almost affectionately unavoidable to hold three, four—even as many as five and six—women in regard—at one and the same time." This is the kind of behavior that later sociological study has confirmed to be very frequent in our rootless society, but it was not being voiced publicly when Dreiser first said it. In none of his accounts did he attempt to give a flattering picture of himself. He spoke of "all my defects of temper and temperament . . . my irritabilities and my sullen moods, as well as my inconsequential gaieties and instabilities of fancy and affection." He referred to himself again and again as "changeful" and "uncertain." Unlike Witla, who finally begot a child, Dreiser—on the testimony of those best able to say—would seem to have been sterile. His continually restless desire to know more and more women may have been a product of basic insecurity, of an almost desperate need to keep on proving himself.

As far as his work was concerned, he never managed to make a fully affecting expression of the passion that had consumed him. What we observed of the trilogy is true again in *The "Genius."* Angela, though presented far too prolixly, is real in her disappointments and defects; but the others, and especially Suzanne—the ultimate in "the beauty of eighteen"—are abstract monsters of unreality. Dreiser seems to have paid the price for his promiscuity in a progressive blunting of his sensibility. His Berenice Flemings and Suzanne Dales are his worst failures, stereotyped "ideals" with no more living differentiation than they would have had in the cheapest magazines.

Nevertheless the historical need for *The "Genius"* may be estimated by the storm that rose against it. In the summer of 1916, after the book had been out for nearly a year, the minister of a Baptist church in Cincinnati—who had been told about it by an unidentified person on the telephone—in turn informed the Western Society for the Prevention of Vice. This group promptly declared that the novel contained seventy-five "lewd" and seventeen "profane" passages, and filed a complaint with the comparable society in New York, of which John S. Sumner was the secretary. His procedure, which has since become notorious, was to intimidate the publisher by threatening that, unless the book was immediately withdrawn from circulation, criminal charges would be brought.

At this remove it is hardly necessary to go into the detailed story of the censorship beyond its significance for

Dreiser's career and for the state of American literature. Dreiser had already encountered another threat of trouble over the publication of *The Titan* when Harper, after the book was already set up, decided not to issue it. Their reason was not made explicit, but they seem suddenly to have feared libel, or the pressure of financiers upon whose good will they were dependent; and objections were raised in particular by one member of the firm who was a friend of the prototype of Berenice Fleming. Dreiser found another publisher, though only after several other rejections. *The Titan* was issued by the American representative of John Lane, and no trouble ensued.

When the storm broke over *The "Genius,"* Dreiser could now fight back, as he had been in no position to do at the time of *Sister Carrie*; but this involved another great waste of energy. Sumner declared that he was looking at the book "from the standpoint of its effect on female readers of immature mind." The itemized list of "profanity" had nothing more to show than some very widely scattered "Gods" and "damns." That of "lewdness" found its exhibits in such passages as the one in which Witla as a young art student was moved "by a great warm-tinted nude by Bouguereau"; in his kissing one of his girls on "her mouth and her neck"; in the remark that Angela and Witla, in their desperate effort to bridge their differences, had flung themselves into excessive sexual "indulgence"—though the intent of this remark was to indicate what undermined their marriage.

Mencken, whatever his dissatisfaction with *The "Genius,"* was at his most vigorous in championing Dreiser in this situation. He was tireless in circulating a protest to the effect that "an attack by irresponsible and arbitrary persons upon an author of such manifest sincerity and such high accomplishments must inevitably do great damage to the freedom of letters in the United States." The eventual signatures to this protest reads almost like a roll call of the newly emerging talents of value, including—beyond Dreiser's own friends—Edwin Arlington Robinson, Willa Cather, Amy Lowell, Robert Frost, and Ezra Pound. Some of the older generation also subscribed, like E. W. Howe and Mary Wilkins Freeman, though Howells refused on the ground that he had not read *The "Genius"*; and many of the more respectable editorial and academic figures refused to become involved. But the real enemy was the new sophisticate, as represented by Henry Sydnor Harrison, the then well-known author of *Queed* and *V.V.'s Eyes*, who began: "I cannot say whether *The "Genius"* is decent or indecent until I have read it . . . something I am unable or unwilling to do." He went on to say that since Dreiser held the philistines in contempt, he ought hardly to mind if the feeling was mutual, and that after all he could take satisfaction in "the distinguished example of Flaubert." He concluded: "You see I am saying that it seems to me Mr. Dreiser has fared very well."

This has seemed worth quoting as a sample of the fancy talk that can always deflect attention from the seriousness of a struggle like Dreiser's. Others hinted, as their successors have in subsequent cases, that the whole suppression was "a piece of very shrewd advertising." They overlooked the economic facts at the base of Dreiser's situation. The total sales of *Jennie Gerhardt* and *The Financier*, which had gone the best, had not yet netted him much beyond five thousand dollars. He was not talking beside the point when he said in his own defense: "The rich strike the poor at every turn; the poor defend themselves and further their lives by all the tricks which stark necessity can conceive. No inalienable right keeps the average cost of living from rising steadily while most of the salaries of our idealistic Americans are stationary. No inalienable right has ever yet prevented the strong from either tricking or browbeating the weak. . . . Personally, my quarrel is with America's quarrel with original thought."

Despite the protest, John Lane still did not dare risk selling the book. His firm agreed that Dreiser should bring suit in order that they might find out where they stood with the law. But when, after the usual delays, the case was finally heard in the Appellate Court in 1918, the court declared that giving advisory judgments was not its function, and that there was no real case before it since Sumner had only threatened and no criminal action had been instigated. This took the matter back to where it had started, and *The "Genius"* remained in the publisher's warehouse for five years more. Then Horace Liveright ventured to bring it out. The climate of opinion had changed considerably by 1923, and the sale was not interfered with.

Dreiser had played the most substantial part he could to effect this change by refusing to yield an inch, and by keeping up the attack in such essays as "Neurotic America and the Sex Impulse" and "Life, Art, and America." Sherwood Anderson read the latter in *The Seven Arts* and wrote: "It sets forth as nothing else I have ever read has set forth the complete and terrible fact of the wall, in the shadow of which American artists must work. To many of us here in America the one really hopeful note in our time is your own stout figure pounding at the wall. Our hats off to you, Captain." He followed this up with an essay in praise of Dreiser called "An Apology for Crudity," in which he dwelt on the necessity even of Dreiser's passages of brute ugliness if the real nature of contemporary America was to be captured.

The suppression had at least served to let Dreiser know more completely where he stood with those he valued. By 1915 he was settled in a small studio apartment on Tenth Street, and was seeing both the writers and the political thinkers who were then making Greenwich Village their center. Several of the most detailed descriptions of him date from this time when he was in the habit of asking people in for the evening. These parties often started off very stiffly, since Dreiser had no ready gifts as a host, and (as Dell reported) "no small talk except a few joshing sillinesses." Nearly everyone remarked on his inveterate habit of rocking moodily while he folded his handkerchief into the smallest possible square, and then unfolded it and began again. Arthur Davison Ficke spoke of his "large laboring inexpressive face." Others observed that when he laughed, he guffawed, and at those moments his eyes "appeared to glance anything but humor—rather depression, discouragement at mankind." Only occasionaly did someone note "the domed forehead . . . the curiously long, beautiful hands." Ernest Boyd summed up his impression of Dreiser on these evenings: "Out of all those laborious platitudes on wealth and art and sex and economics, those proofs of technical helplessness in the art of writing, there emerged a picture of a man of unspoiled sensitiveness to the storm and stress of Nature, of an elemental energy and passionate desire to understand."

Even before *The "Genius"* was attacked, Dreiser's admirers were speaking of him more and more frequently as "our greatest writer." He was beginning to be in a position to be of help to others, and was instrumental in finding a publisher for the *Spoon River Anthology* and for *Windy McPherson's Son*. Anderson had sent him his manuscript before they had ever met; and Masters wrote: "I wish you would give me your opinion of these imagiste ventures into rural delineations of fate and sorrow." Their common concern with the fate that overwhelms men was what made the deepest bond between these two. In Dreiser's view Masters became now *the* American poet since Whitman. He was to admire Sandburg's *Chicago Poems*, but never to feel in them the same depth.

Masters wrote two poems about Dreiser, and included one of them among the Spoon River figures as "Theodore, the Poet." He spoke more incisively in the other, calling Dreiser "Fearless, grim, compassionate and hateful," "Disordered, yet with a passion for order," and "Self-mastered and beyond friendship." Anderson summed up his impression a few years later when dedicating *Horses and Men* to him. He said that Dreiser personified "something gray and bleak and hurtful, that has been in the world perhaps forever." He also stated his great debt: "The prose writers in America who follow Dreiser will have much to do that he has never done. Their road is long but, because of him, those who follow will never have to face the road through the wilderness of Puritan denial, the road that Dreiser faced alone." Dreiser and Anderson saw each other seldom, but they remained emotionally close. Dreiser spoke of Anderson's being essentially a poet in the tenderness of his best work, and told him that he had "a kindly and beautiful mind."

But Dreiser was often beyond friendship in his craggy, dour, and sometimes suspicious aloofness. The friend he valued most steadily through the years was John Cowper Powys, who was frequently in America. Powys never lost his perception of a mysterious, even enigmatic, largeness in Dreiser's personality; and he believed that this was revealed in his fiction through Dreiser's way of giving the reader a sense not so much of individuals as of universal force, "the mass and weight of the stupendous life-tide." In his review of *The "Genius"* Powys contended that "nobody in the Dreiser-world" is "protected" from this force, "nobody is so privileged. The great stream sweeps them all forward, sweeps them all away; and not they, but It, must be regarded as the hero of the tale."

This widens out what Randolph Bourne felt, expressing the fullest range of Dreiser's power as sensed by his contemporaries. Dreiser added a few strokes of his own to the portrait we have been sketching of him in mid-career. He had said in *A Traveler at Forty*: "There is in me the spirit of a lonely child" that "cries when it is frightened; and then there is a coarse, vulgar exterior which fronts the world defiantly and bids all and sundry go to the devil." Dorothy Dudley, who first met him in 1916, thought of him as essentially three men: the competitor, brusque and even bullying and cruel; the warm if intermittent companion; and the creative recluse. In *A Hoosier Holiday*, the account of a motor trip he took in the summer of 1915, the second of these was dominant. His curiosity was intensely alive as he revisited the places of his childhood. He was caught out of himself into a renewed fondness for people: "Dear, crude, asinine, illusioned Americans! How I love them!" He now could feel that notwithstanding all he could "sum up against America, it was actually better than Europe"—primarily through its zest. When he thought of its cultural ignorances, to be sure, he wrote some passages in Menckenese and branded the society as one of "mush-heads and loons." But his basic mood was one of satisfaction with "this tremendous bubbling Republic," with this easy-paced land of the Middle West, even though he did not think that it could survive in its illusions. This was hardly his habitual mood of social comment, but here he was the man who could say: "I have seen a great many things in my time, done a lot of dull ones, suffered intense shames, disgraces and privations, but all taken into account and notwithstanding, I would gladly be born again and do it all over, so much have I loved the life I have been permitted to live."

The Essential Tragedy
of Life

I T IS hard to say how much the suppression of *The
"Genius"* had to do with keeping Dreiser from completing another novel for nearly a decade. He already had
plans for *The Bulwark*, whose title was ironic inasmuch as
the theme was the corroding and destructive effect of the
world upon a late-nineteenth-century Philadelphia Quaker
and his family. But though this was announced for publication in 1916, Dreiser soon discontinued work on it. By
contrast with the years after *Sister Carrie*, however, this
time he was in full pursuit of many other projects, several
of which had developed before his trouble with the censors.
Early in 1915 he applied to the New York Public Library
for a study in which he could do some reading in chemistry
and physics, a sign of the deepening interest in science that
was to possess him for the rest of his life. He was also writing some poems in free verse. His return to Indiana led him
into planning a more detailed autobiography. But before
this—in the spring of 1913, while still engaged on *The Titan*—he had written his first one-act play, "The Girl in
the Coffin."

He had persisted in his earliest belief that the dramatic

form was the "most natural" for him, but his trying his hand at it now may have been stimulated by his contact with the Little Theater in Chicago. In the summer of 1914 he was to write five of his other six short plays "of the Natural and the Supernatural," and he added "Old Rag-picker" a year later. The one of these that comes closest to bearing out his conviction that he had a gift for this form, and one of the few to reach the stage, was "The Girl in the Coffin," produced by the Washington Square Players. It pictures a labor organizer's house at the time of a textile strike. The organizer, William Magnet, is badly shaken by the death of his daughter who, unmarried, has died of an abortion. He refuses to take any further part in the strike, though this is the night of the crucial meeting. Faced by the hard-bitten leader from the outside, John Ferguson, whom he has admired greatly, he still refuses, against every plea that his responsibility to his fellow workmen is beyond any personal sorrow. Then Ferguson says: "You are not the only man in this town tonight whose hopes are lying in a coffin," and goes on to tell Magnet that he (Ferguson) has lost the girl he loved, the girl he could not marry because he was badly married, the girl to whom he was not even faithful and yet whom he loved. His strong controlled final speech affirms how none the less he will keep on fighting with the men. At this Magnet quietly walks out, to the meeting. Ferguson follows, after going over to the coffin, for here—unknown to Magnet and to the audience until this moment—was the girl Ferguson had loved. The tension holds, and Masters was accurate in observing: "There's a naked horror, Greek in its starkness, of the coffin in the room. . . . What a passion of pity you have!"

Dreiser's favorite among these plays was one of the "supernatural," "Laughing Gas," concerning which he wrote
Mencken: "Supremely the best—personally I think the best
thing I ever did." But here he was badly mistaken. His effort to dramatize the speculations of a famous physician
who, while anesthetized, believes that he is reaching beyond the margins of consciousness, has hardly any substance. The reason why Dreiser saw so much in it must
have been that it was based on an experience of his own,
which had deepened his sense of the mystery of the im-
pinging cosmos. The other "supernatural" plays, no more
substantial, remind us that he was throughout his life
strongly haunted by premonitions and omens. "Old Rag-
picker," the starkest of the "natural" plays, presents a helpless old man, formerly well-to-do, picking about in garbage
cans on a New York street; but it is hardly more than a
genre sketch.

In the fall of 1916, in the midst of the attack on *The
"Genius,"* Dreiser undertook his one full-length play, *The
Hand of the Potter*. The epigraph from Omar Khayyám,
"What! did the Hand then of the Potter shake?" may seem
very dated now. But for Dreiser it linked with his earliest
image of an artist at work, the Indiana potter at his wheel.
The idea that engaged him in this play is akin to the one
he was to develop in *An American Tragedy*, that of a
young man helpless before his impulses. Here he is Isadore
Berchansky, the twenty-one-year-old son of impoverished
lower East Side immigrant parents, "so badly composed
chemically that he seems never to be of one mood," with
a deformed left shoulder that twitches continually, and
with an uncontrollable attraction to young girls. He has
only recently finished two years in prison for one attack;

but now, left alone in the tenement for a short time, he assaults and then murders a neighbor's child of eleven. Dreiser apparently did not reckon at all with the difference between tragic material and a pathological case history. He carried the play relentlessly to Isadore's detection, with the most effectively built scene the one before the grand jury where the boy's father, trying hopelessly to shield him, finally breaks down and confesses, insisting: "He could not help it. He is not right." The boy himself, still hiding out, goes to his miserable suicide with the same refrain: "I couldn't help it, could I? I didn't make myself, did I?" Dreiser's determination to establish the social judgment that Isadore is sick rather than willfully guilty overlooked the cardinal fact that the destruction of the helplessly unfit affords none of the struggle needed to involve an audience's sympathy. By the time he wrote *An American Tragedy* his brooding over the problem of justice and mercy had found a far more adequate chain of circumstances.

But he believed that in this play he had "touched the exposed nerve of life," and Masters agreed in finding it "very powerful." On the other hand, Mencken, to whom he also sent the manuscript, opened against it the strongest attack he could. He was thinking primarily of the effect its publication would have upon the fight for *The "Genius"*: "Nothing is more abhorrent to the average man than sexual perversion. He would roar against it in the theater. . . . Resisting with justice the imbecilities of the Comstocks, you unconsciously fly to an extreme, and demand a degree of freedom that is obviously impossible. . . . Fully half of the signers of the Protest, painfully seduced into signing by all sorts of artifices, will demand that their names be taken off. . . . Its publication would lose you your own case, forfeit the respect of all intelligent persons, and make every man who has labored on the protest look like an ass."

Dreiser's defense was upon what seemed to him far more basic grounds: "When you . . . tell me what I can or cannot put on the stage, what the artistic or moral limitations of the stage are and what the American people will stand for, you may be well within your critical rights but my answer is that I have more respect for my own judgment in this matter than I have for yours. In other words your limitations are not mine. . . . You write as if you thought I were entering on a defense of perversion. . . . If you would look at the title page you would see it labelled a *tragedy*. What has tragedy ever illuminated—unless it is the inscrutability of life and its forces and its accidents. . . . Tragedy is tragedy and I will go where I please for my subject. If I fail ridiculously in the execution let the public and the critics kick me out. They will anyhow. But so long as I have an adequate possession of my senses current convention will not dictate to me where I shall look for art. . . . My inner instincts and passions and pities are going to instruct me."

However misconceived and inadequate *The Hand of the Potter*, Dreiser's "passions and pities" were the sources that kept his work alive. He had been aware for some time of his growing divergence from Mencken. He had written him the year before about *The Smart Set*: "Under you and Nathan the thing seems to have tamed down to a light non-disturbing period[ical] of persiflage and badinage. . . . Really the thing is too debonair, too Broadway-esque, too full of 'josh' and 'kid,' like a Broadway and 42 Street curb actor. Everything, apparently, is to be done with a light, aloof touch, which to me is good but like a diet of soufflé." He urged him to take a lead from Reedy or from *The Masses* ("There are splendid indictments to be drawn of a score of things right now"). He urged him also to print Masters and Vachel Lindsay and some translations of Chekhov instead of so much froth.

Mencken was, of course, right in what he foresaw would happen to *The Hand of the Potter*. Dreiser could find no producer or publisher for it until Liveright took over all his work at the close of the First World War, and issued the play in 1919. A belated production by the Provincetown Players in 1921 had no success. In the meantime Dreiser was still not far from the threat of poverty. It had taken him over three years to place "The Lost Phoebe" (from 1912 to 1916), which has since been the most frequently reprinted of all his short stories. Yet, however uncertain their possibilities of publication, short pieces seemed to afford at this time his best chance to keep going. *Free and Other Stories* (1918) was his first collection, and the first of his books to be handled by Horace Liveright's new firm, in the arrangement that was to prove for the next dozen years more profitable than any Dreiser had previously known.

Of the eleven stories that he now presented, four, as we know, dated back to the very beginning of his career. "The Lost Phoebe" is in a different vein from any of those. Located in the remote pre-industrial countryside which Dreiser dealt with only rarely, it records the hallucination of an old man whose wife has died after their half-century of marriage. Out of his unendurable loneliness he persuades himself that she is not really dead, that she has left him for being too querulous, but that he can find her and bring her back. The spectral quality of his pursuit in the "sad greenish-white" moonlight is brought out by some of Dreiser's most sensitive descriptions. The allegorical undertone is the most affecting in that the shining bird, latent in the wife's name, is never directly mentioned. The story is Dreiser's most poetic, not at all sentimentalized but entirely tender, as the moon leads the old man, still calling his "Phoebe," to his death over a cliff where he is sure that he sees her below "among a silvery bed of apple trees."

The other very impressive story is "The Second Choice," more characteristic of Dreiser in the bleak bareness with which it treats the situation of a working-class girl who, swept off her feet by the temporary attentions of a far more attractive man, has broken off her relations with the dull plodding clerk she was going to marry. But as she finds herself in turn left behind, she knows that she must face what seems to be destined for her. She feels that her life is a failure, but Dreiser's emphasis is on the way she picks up its old strands again, if with quiet desperation.

In both these stories Dreiser had managed his own kind of unostentatious plot; but when he tried, in "Will You Walk Into My Parlor?", the unexpected trick ending, so dear to the magazines, of the account of how a persistent girl finally contrived to frame a publicist during a political campaign, the result was dismally flat. Another way—the most fundamental way in which Dreiser could go wrong —is what vitiates the effect of the title-story. This consists of the thoughts of a sixty-year-old architect who has wanted to be free of his wife. But as he keeps ponderously asking, "Why had his life been so hard?", pity has shifted into self-pity, and we cannot be greatly moved. This failure points out again how important it was for Dreiser to project his feelings away from himself, away from the purely subjective realm in which he could lose his sense of proportion, into objective solidity.

Far more native to his gifts than contrived stories was the material he collected next, in *Twelve Men* (1919). We have already looked at the most powerful of these sketches, since they constitute some of his most essential autobiography. They also possess his finest and most massive objectivity, as he presents the men for themselves, not just in relation to himself. He thought of the later companion volume, *A Gallery of Women* (1929), as far bolder. But once again his skills in differentiation deserted him when he tried to handle details that must have seemed to him more intimate, and none of those portraits have anything of the definitive likeness possessed by those of Paul or Peter McCord or Muldoon or Burke.

In arranging this book, Dreiser put last one of his earliest sketches, that of Louis Sontag, an illustrator whom he had known during his own first days in New York, and who had then died with all his ambitions unfulfilled. Dreiser's reason for this arrangement may well have been that it enabled him to end with a passage that could serve as an appropriate finale for the whole book, and that also attained the volume of feeling which he had striven for but never encompassed in his verse: "We toil so much, we dream so richly, we hasten so fast, and lo! the green door is opened. We are through it, and its grassy surface has sealed us for ever from all which apparently we so much crave—even as, breathlessly, we are still running."

A year later he published his first group of the philosophical essays that would thereafter occupy a larger and larger share of his attention. He called this book by the deliberately incongruous title, *Hey-rub-a-dub-dub*, as though to suggest the call of a circus barker. When asked what he meant, he said: "Just that: That life—like the title . . . is without meaning and has no objective." But his subtitle embodied his dominant theme: "A Book of the Mystery and Wonder and Terror of Life." The opening essay is his most condensed expression of attitudes that are at the heart of all his novels. Once again he gave them a fictional projection, alleging that they were "taken from the notes of the late John Paradiso." This was the name of Dreiser's first employer in his dish-washing job in Chicago; but here he has placed him in New Jersey, in a poor neighborhood of Poles and Hungarians, just across the river from the great city upon which Dreiser had never ceased to brood. This closeness to and yet distance from the dreams of success give the right setting for his reflections: "I am one of those curious persons who cannot make up their minds about anything. . . . I sit here and read and read, when I have time, wondering." His thoughts are those we have found latent or expressed throughout Dreiser's work. He does not pretend to "understand life," though he likes it for all the fine dramatic spectacles it presents. He cannot see why people try to cling to fixed moral schemes. His observation and experience have led him "to believe that there is scarcely a so-called 'sane,' right, merciful, true, just solution to anything"; that everything is the prey of processes that are "stark, relentless, brutal." He can find nothing to assuage his "vaulting egotism," and yet he perceives intermittently a cosmic beauty in nature, "all too frail perhaps against the endless drag toward nothingness, but still lovely and comforting."

This is not a philosophy, but only fragments of one, and

Dreiser himself was not to remain satisfied with it. It is significant that the phrase most frequently quoted from this essay to epitomize Dreiser's approach to life—"My pride in a sturdy, passive acceptance of things"—is here most clearly realized in Vaclav Melka, a saloon keeper indifferent to everything outside his immediate sphere. Dreiser had often observed the apathy of the new American city dweller. When John Paradiso asked the man who ran the tobacco store on the corner what he thought about the Colorado mining troubles, he replied: "I never read de papers," and added: "I doaned belong to no church. I doaned mix in no politics, neider." Dreiser's own openness to experience, whatever its dismaying confusions, would lead him farther into realms both of philosophy and of politics than he had yet ventured.

This first book of essays included the one on "Change," and his various pieces on our national character as revealed by the disproportion between our activities in business and in the arts. Most revelatory of the main direction his thought was to take during the next few years was "The Essential Tragedy of Life." He deemed this to consist in man's consciousness of the immense forces beyond his control, and of the basic fact that he does not use these forces, but is used by them. This would be the leading motive in his presentation of the tragedy of Clyde Griffiths.

By the time his essays had come out Dreiser was in California, where he had gone to recover from the accident of being run down by an automobile in Columbus Circle. He lived in Los Angeles for three years, and formed there the most enduring relationship of his life. This was with Helen Richardson, a young actress, who had much of the generosity and devotion of a Jennie Gerhardt. Since his wife would not agree to a divorce, Dreiser and Helen were not able to marry until after Sallie's death, which occurred in 1942.

Dreiser also made some new friendships in California, particularly with George Sterling and with the critic George Douglas. As usual, no matter where he was living, he was writing most of the time. The bulk of the stories to be included in *Chains* (1927) belong to these years, as do many of the sketches for *A Gallery of Women*. He also completed *A Book about Myself* (1922), which on being reprinted in 1931 was called *Newspaper Days*, and collected his earlier sketches of New York in *The Color of a Great City* (1923). This came out just after his return east. By then he had already written twenty chapters of a big novel he was calling *Mirage*. The reason for this title would appear to lie in his statement that life is "a complete illusion or mirage which changes and so escapes and eludes one at every point."

Of Crime and Punishment

FOR American fiction, the nineteen-twenties inaugurated a more flourishing period than any Dreiser had previously known. Several of his near contemporaries were coming into their own with a wider public. His most devoted followers, especially Sherwood Anderson, were growing up around him. Among the many new talents which made this decade one of the richest in our literary history, both realists like Sinclair Lewis and naturalists like Dos Passos were conscious of how much Dreiser had helped to prepare their way. It is more surprising to find Scott Fitzgerald saying, at the dawn of his own career: "I consider H. L. Mencken and Theodore Dreiser the greatest men living in the country today."

Dreiser took a varying and complex attitude towards the dominant mood of the 'twenties. He joined in their sweeping arraignment of the past and present inadequacies of American culture, and said flatly: "We are not an artistic nation. All we care about is to be rich and powerful." But this conviction did not lead him, as it did so many younger artists, to flight and exile. The roots of his own life were now inextricably intertwined with half a century of American experience, and, though he noted that much he had gone through had been "inimical to mental freedom and artistic energy," he still could declare America to be "as satisfying to me, as stimulating, I am sure, as Russia ever was to Tolstoy or Dostoevsky . . . or France to Flaubert or de Maupassant."

These examples indicate his realization—out of a wider range of reference than he had previously possessed—that the artist's adjustment to society is never likely to be easy. He was sympathetic with social protest, but reaffirmed his belief that the greatest writers "are not concerned with social amelioration as an end or a motive. Rather their purpose is to present life in the round, good, bad, and indifferent, alike, without thought of change and without hope of improvement. They paint the thing as it is, leaving change to nature or to others." In an introduction to a new edition of *Tono-Bungay* he strongly preferred Wells the novelist to Wells the reformer. This preference was naturally colored by Dreiser's own recurrent doubts of all efforts to order the world. "As I see him," he stated again in this introduction, "man is much more led or pushed than he is leading or pushing."

He admired the new fiction for the frankness of its record, yet in another twist of mood he saw a serious limitation in its lack of "exaltation." He was also puzzled by the fact that so many of this next generation of realists wanted "to indict life, not picture it in its ordinary beauty. . . . What is lacking in the experience of these young writers to make them think there is no beauty?" By observing where Dreiser believed "beauty" and "exaltation" were now to be found, we may begin to catch the tone of the long novel upon which he was at work and which he hoped would provide what the decade was missing. Beauty did not exist for him in delicate or fragile isolation. He described his characteristic associations with it when he voiced his appreciation of the essays of Llewellyn Powys: "They are so serious, so pathetic, so—in the main—sombre and so beautiful. They are so full of a genuine understanding of life and of a kind of sane sorrow because of the fact that in general things are so necessitous, so hopeless, and so un-rewarded. And yet there is a courageous and hence im-pressive joy in the amazing and ebullient beauty that in-forms the necessitous and inexplicable and unescapable process which we know as living."

Beauty was to be seized at the heart of tragedy, as was also exaltation: "If there are all the chain cigar stores, chain drug stores, haberdasheries, movie theatres, and big hotels in Manhattan to describe, here are also Hell, Heaven, and Purgatory of the soul." But contemporary writers, held too close by the details of surface description, "rarely climb any such heights as Dante climbed to look out over the tre-mendous waste of lives." Dreiser had none of the firmness of vision to emulate even from afar *The Divine Comedy*. But he must have been conscious of the fact that he was summoning up all his resources when he changed the title of his novel from *Mirage* to *An American Tragedy*. In an interview in 1921, in which he looked back to his situation at the time of *Sister Carrie*, he revealed the point of view that was to be dominant in his treatment of Clyde Grif-fiths: "I never can and never want to bring myself to the place where I can ignore the sensitive and seeking individ-ual in his pitiful struggle with nature—with his enormous urges and his pathetic equipment."

Dreiser worked longer and more steadily upon this novel

· 189 ·

than upon any of his others. This concentration was made possible by the fact that Liveright—who had now brought all his works together under one imprint and in 1923 had reissued *The "Genius"*—was providing him with a four-thousand-dollar annual drawing account. He wrote, as always, with great uncertainty and difficulty. But he had chosen his subject deliberately, and was sure that it was not only right for what he wanted to say, but also very typical of American life. When he had revisited Terre Haute in 1915, he had stayed at the same hotel to which his mother had once come looking for work. He recalled how his brother Rome used sometimes to put on the best clothes he had and idle outside the doorway with a toothpick in his mouth to give the impression that he had just dined there. Looking around the midnight grill, Dreiser watched those the community would call "our most successful men," men "of a solid, resonant, generative materiality. The flare of the cloth of their suits! The blaze of their skins and eyes! The hardy, animal implication of their eyes!" These were lesser Cowperwoods, and Dreiser continued to be attracted by them.

"But," he went on, "what interested me more, and this was sad too, were the tribes and shoals of the incomplete, the botched, the semi-articulate, all hungry and helpless, who never get to come to a place like this at all—who yearn for a taste of this show and flare and never attain to the least taste of it." These were the opposites of Cowperwood, of Dreiser's American version of the surviving fittest. From these other ranks he was to pick Clyde Griffiths, but he would give him a taste of the wealth from which he was excluded, and the weak boy, more sensitive than most and thus more helpless, would be destroyed by it.

In one sense, Dreiser was taking one of the stock legends

of American behavior and reversing its happy ending. After the novel's appearance in 1925 he said: "The type of life that produced it has not changed. For years I have been arrested in stories and plays by the poor young man who marries the rich man's daughter. I have had many letters from people who wrote: 'Clyde Griffiths might have been me.'"

He was also writing a documentary novel, as he did in his study of the businessman. But here the core of his material was even more public—not the story of financial operations that a Yerkes would keep as hidden as he could, but what everybody was reading in the newspapers, indeed, the favorite drama of the American people: the story of a murder trial. After pondering several other cases he chose for his document the drowning of Grace Brown by Chester Gillette in Moose Lake, Herkimer County, New York, in 1906. Dreiser's center of interest, to be sure, was not in crime and its detection, but in contemplating a victim of the contemporary American dream. Clyde Griffiths' aspirations to rise in the world, to be a success as measured by money and social position, were those stimulated and sanctioned by twentieth-century capitalist society, and Dreiser instinctively moved his climax, without specifying any dates, into the showy period after the First World War. Before the glittering possibility of marrying Sondra Finchley had flashed upon him, Clyde had become involved, out of his loneliness and repression, in an affair with the mill girl Roberta Alden. If he had had some money of his own, he might have handled the unlooked-for consequence— Roberta's pregnancy—as the harder and more experienced young men of the social set knew how to. But Clyde was caught, and thrashed about in a hopeless effort to escape.

What Dreiser studied was the sexual and social forces that overpowered Clyde and swept him before them until, seeing no way out, in his shallow immaturity he finally plotted murder. Yet Roberta's actual death was accidental, since the boat into which Clyde lured her upon the lake overturned at a moment when he had not willed it. The ultimate range of Dreiser's theme thereby became the terrible and baffling problem of justice.

His chief addition to his sources was his detailed presentation, in the first of the three books of his novel, of Clyde's background. The Gillette family, though not wealthy, were not really poor. But Dreiser, in order to carry Clyde's actions beyond the sphere of any merely temperamental aberration, immersed the Griffiths family in poverty as extreme as his own youth had known. As a result, Clyde's world, from the time we first see him as a boy of twelve until his death, is portrayed with a more deliberate and more detailed thoroughness than that of any of Dreiser's other characters. Dreiser shows him as always worked upon by his environment and circumstances, even to the point of being tempted to murder by coming across a newspaper account of a drowning.

In the opening scene he is an unwilling participant in the street service conducted by his preacher father in connection with the itinerant Bible mission he runs. For this vague impractical father Dreiser drew in part upon Asa Conklin, his employer in his first job after his year at college, who had been equally vague and impractical in his schemes for promoting real estate. The emotional center of the Griffiths family is Clyde's mother, who buoys up her husband by her wholehearted if ignorant faith. But Clyde is from the start alien to their values. He observes that his parents are forever proclaiming the care of God for all, and yet they are always "hard up": "Plainly there was something wrong somewhere." Beginning in this fashion Dreiser makes a sustained contrast between the professed and the actual, as it strikes a boy who will have little regular education and no accurate training for anything.

Each successive episode is designed by Dreiser for its bearing upon Clyde's final tragedy. For instance, his older sister Esta, as tired of the dreariness of their life as he is ("dreary" is one of the recurrent key words here), runs away with a lover. In spite of his parents' grief, Clyde, now in his adolescence, cannot see that "her going was such a calamity, not from the *going* point of view at any rate." Then she is deserted and comes back, and Clyde reflects that this is typical of everything that happens in the family, of their repeated rhythm of failure. But as she bears her illegitimate child, Clyde cannot share in the stock emotion of blaming the whole affair upon the seducer. His confused mixture of feelings foreshadows what they will be in his own affair with Roberta.

The section of this first book that has been praised most often is where Dreiser evokes the splendor for which Clyde longs by making him a bell-hop in the Green-Davidson in Kansas City. The vast luxury hotel is a peculiarly fitting symbol for the glamour and the waste of the modern American city, as Henry James had observed in *The American Scene*. Dreiser's way of conveying its spell over Clyde is one of the most matured examples of his method. He is more detached than when he wrote *Sister Carrie*. He can now judge as "gauche" all the senseless overfurnishing which is "without the saving grace of either simplicity or necessity." But his richly stored memory can create to the full Clyde's own amazement and awe at "this perfectly marvellous-marvellous realm." Dreiser is so sympathetically involved with how everything here would strike Clyde's starved imagination that he can take us through the routine of a bell-hop's day as though, once again, it were something out of *The Arabian Nights*. The downpour of small change into his hand "seemed fantastic, Aladdinish really." Dreiser can make us feel what Clyde feels, even through the trite image Clyde uses when complimenting his first girl friend Hortense: " 'An' your eyes are just like soft, black velvet,' he persisted eagerly. 'They're wonderful.' He was thinking of an alcove in the Green-Davidson hung with black velvet."

But the main reason why Dreiser can make us feel touched by Clyde's feelings is that he is aware of how pathetic they really are. For Clyde this hotel is the actual world in contrast with his family's shakily based ideal. But Dreiser, with a firmness of balance he had never quite possessed before, can let us sense at the same time how hopelessly wrong Clyde is in believing that these surroundings mark "a social superiority almost unbelievable." Dreiser observes that here was the "most dangerous" environment for the boy's temperament that could have been found. He was so "insanely eager for all the pleasures which he imagined he saw swirling around him." His "none-too-discerning" mind could so easily be convinced that the chief end of life was having and spending money.

This first book ends with Clyde's initial disaster. A car in which he is riding with a group of the other bell-hops and their girls runs down a child; and Clyde, knowing that the scandal will cost him his job, decides to skip out of town. We see him next three years later, twenty now and very cautious, working at the Union League Club in Chicago. Here by chance he encounters the uncle whom he had envisaged distantly as a "kind of Croesus," Samuel Griffiths, a collar manufacturer of Lycurgus, New York. He is favorably impressed by Clyde's quiet good looks, and, feeling also some compunction over his previous neglect of his brother's family, he listens to the young man's request that he be given an opportunity to make his way in the mill. The shift to an upstate New York town of twenty-five thousand affords Dreiser another sphere in which to demonstrate how completely he has worked out the details of the world in which he has placed Clyde.

He has studied once again the gradations of the economic and social scale. Though secretly somewhat awed by the bigger men he meets in Chicago, in Lycurgus Samuel Griffiths is at the top. The self-made founder of his own business, he already represents a degree of solid conservatism not yet attained by the families of even newer enterprises, such as the Finchley Electric Sweepers. Dreiser also makes a telling contrast between Mr. Griffiths, who is in general tolerant and forbearing, and his son Gilbert, who is self-centered, vain, and meanly arrogant. This is the same kind of difference Dreiser noted in *Jennie Gerhardt* between Archibald and Robert Kane. Eisenstein, whose script for a picture based on *An American Tragedy* was not what Paramount wanted, seized upon the significance of the contrast. He saw that in Mr. Griffiths "there still prevails the patriarchal democratic spirit of the fathers, who have not forgotten how they themselves came to the town in rags to make their fortunes. The succeeding generation is already approximating to a money aristocracy; and in this connection it is interesting to note the difference in attitude towards Clyde adopted by his uncle and his cousin respectively." Mr. Griffiths takes it for granted that Clyde should have his chance; Gilbert regards him as an interloper who should be kept out of their inner circle.

Another telling contrast, which occupies Clyde's thoughts through most of the long second book, is between Roberta and Sondra. Roberta is like Clyde in that her whole youth has been grounded in poverty. She has come from her father's farm to work in the mill, afflicted by the same "virus of ambition and unrest" that afflicts Clyde. Until she meets him she still feels herself terribly alone. And when he, as the foreman of the shop in which she is working, begins to show an interest in her, she looks up to him as someone far outside her sphere. This is one of Dreiser's most effective strokes in pointing out the successive rungs of insecurity. For Clyde at this moment is aware that he has not really been accepted by Sondra's family and that he stands firmly nowhere.

The developing relationship betwen them, entered upon with misgivings by both, is handled with Dreiser's greatest tenderness. He knows how, in their first happiness together, they will feel at the Starlight Amusement Park "a kind of ecstasy all out of proportion to the fragile, gimcrack scene." He is equally in possession of Roberta's whole state of mind from her first deep sense of guilt at yielding herself to Clyde to her agonized realization that she can no longer hold him. The crisis when she discovers that she is going to have a baby, and when Clyde tries in vain to find a doctor who will perform an abortion, is regarded by Dreiser as "an illustration of the enormous handicaps imposed by ignorance, youth, poverty and fear." Dreiser knows Roberta thoroughly, and Clyde's vision of her "steady, accusing, horrified, innocent blue eyes" is likely to remain with the reader as long as anything in the novel.

The contrast with Sondra Finchley is revelatory in more ways than Dreiser seems to have meant it to be. From the first moment Clyde sees her with his cousins, she appears to him "as smart and vain and sweet a girl" as he has ever laid eyes on. These curiously mixed adjectives suggest the quality of the social group in which she is at the center, a faster-moving and more stylish group than is quite approved by the rather conservative Griffiths. Clyde reads about her avidly in the society columns until she decides one day to take him up "as a lark," partly because she realizes how much this will irritate his cousin Gilbert. At this point Clyde determines to break off with Roberta, only to discover that it is already too late. Sondra soon realizes that she is really attracted by Clyde. She is flattered at first by his doglike devotion, but gradually responds to an intensity in him beyond that of the college boys she is used to. But what Clyde finds in his "baby-talking girl" is what Dreiser never manages to convey to us concretely.

Here is the clearest-cut instance of what we have noted recurrently in Dreiser's portrayal of women. He was able to give reality to the kind he had known when he was young. But as soon as he reached above a certain point in the social scale, the details seem superficial and the total effect false. By the mid-nineteen-twenties he had doubtless known many flappers like Sondra, but he still could not make them actual. We therefore have here a strangely double effect. We know what Sondra symbolizes for Clyde, but it is as though we were looking at her from a distance, through the language of the society columns or the eyes of the outsider who does not really understand her. In part this may have been what Dreiser intended. When Clyde attempts to explain at the end the overwhelming fascination Sondra exercised over him, he says: "She seemed to know more than anyone else I ever knew." We have had no evidence of her knowing anything beyond the silliest prattle, and there is the sad irony of Clyde's having been so deluded. But Dreiser's presentation of Sondra is not primarily satirical. He was trying to suggest the social set in its animation as well as its superficiality, and for this he had none of the equipment that was second nature to Scott Fitzgerald. Both words and tune seem wrong this time, and not merely when Sondra coos: "Cantum be happy out here wis Sonda and all these nicey good-baddies?" When Gilbert says, "Spin the big news, Dad," or one of the college boys asks, "Did you hear who is being touted for stroke next year over at Cornell?" we have no illusion that we are listening to possible talk.

The third book, consisting entirely of the trial and its aftermath, raises the chief questions about structure. Dreiser devotes over a hundred thousand words to the account of the trial itself, from the first introduction of the local coroner, leafing through a mail-order catalogue when the telephone rings, to the verdict of guilty. Here the novel becomes documentary in the most literal sense. Many of the lawyers' speeches are based very closely upon what was actually said, and even Roberta's pathetic letters to Clyde, which become the most affecting evidence against him, often reproduce almost verbatim those of Grace Brown. The question, as in all such matters, is what Dreiser made of his sources, and here opinion has been very divided. For some readers interest breaks down under the sheer weight of details; for others the exhaustiveness of Dreiser's treatment is what builds up to an effect of final authority. Eisenstein, for instance, admired the whole novel for being "as broad and shoreless as the Hudson . . . as immense as life itself," and regarded it in its total structure as an "epic of cosmic veracity and objectivity."

It is certainly the most carefully planned of all Dreiser's novels, and though its movement is slow, it advances magisterially from beginning to end. He made use of a simple but effective "framing" device to suggest the bounds of Clyde's world, virtually duplicating his opening and closing chapters. In each he takes us into the deep canyon of a big city on a languorous summer night, and shows us the Griffiths family group lifting their voices in song "against the vast scepticism and apathy of life." He could hardly have produced a more concentrated impression of the overpowering and dwarfing metropolitan desert—of "such walls," as he remarks parenthetically, "as in time may linger as a mere fable." They are no fable here. They are the stone and steel of Kansas City at the beginning, and of San Francisco at the end. But at the end Clyde's place has been taken by Esta's boy, now eight years old.

Dreiser also introduced a few more developed devices of foreshadowing than he had tried before. For example, when Clyde first meets Roberta outside the factory, he invites her out in an amusement park boat, and she asks "Will it be perfectly safe?" Thus is she launched upon the utter insecurity of her relationship with him which will end only when, at a far more distant and deserted spot, she will step down into the boat of her death. A comparable way of causing us to look back to the start is the parting gift to Clyde from another man in the death house, a lawyer who, though a refined intellectual in looks and manner, has been convicted of poisoning an old man of great wealth. He leaves Clyde his copy of *The Arabian Nights*.

But such thematic devices are still sparse in Dreiser's method, and he depends for his dramatic effects primarily upon the kind of bare contrasts he had used in *Sister Carrie*. One of the strongest of these also bears out how, despite the great length of this novel, many of the individual scenes are very compact. In a chapter of only three pages he affords us two glimpses, first by Roberta of Clyde's world, and then by him of hers. Anguished now by the thought that he is going to desert her, Roberta comes along Central Avenue to see him standing beside the car of one of Sondra's friends, and the girl "affectedly posed at the wheel" is for Roberta "an epitome of all the security, luxury, and freedom from responsibility" which are enticing Clyde away. Put side by side with this is Clyde, riding with his new friends, and getting out of the car to ask directions at a farmhouse. He momentarily stops short in his tracks, and Sondra calls, "What's the matter, Clyde? Afraid of the bow-wow?" He has read the name on the mailbox, Titus Alden, and here in this dilapidated and miserable house, and in the threadbare and beaten figure of the man who he knows must be Roberta's father, he sees the typification of everything that he has most wanted to escape, and that now seems to be extending "its gloomy, poverty-stricken arms" to seize him once more. In both these glimpses, incidentally, clothes still play a central symbolical role.

When one moves from smaller to larger scenes, one gets an increasing sense of the rightness of Dreiser's over-all proportions. The quality of spacing is what makes most memorable a kind of effect he had not attempted before, the suggestion of the remoteness from human contact of the lake to which Clyde lures Roberta. He evokes the desolateness of the spot partly by the very slowness with which he takes the two from their secret meeting in Utica to a pleasant resort, and then to a more remote one, and then to Big Bittern. To heighten its unearthly quality he draws also upon the language of fantasy. Clyde has been compelled here as though "some Giant Efrit" had sprung up in his brain. The water itself is "like a huge, black pearl cast by some mighty hand, in anger possibly." Some of these details may seem stock in themselves, but their cumulative effect is to remove Clyde farther and farther from his charted paths of ordinary reality, to numb his mind to the point where Roberta becomes to him "an almost nebulous figure" in "an insubstantial rowboat upon a purely ideational lake." In this way Dreiser builds up our acceptance of the involuntary nature of the catastrophe.

But the large questions still remain: wherein is this novel particularly American, and wherein is it a tragedy? Ten years after the book's appearance, when a boy named Robert Edwards killed a girl in circumstances running closely parallel to those Dreiser had treated, he was asked to be a special reporter at the trial. He also wrote how he had first reached the conclusion that he had found in such a case "the real American tragedy." He went back to his newspaper days when he had begun to observe the consuming passion of his time to be the desire for wealth. He recalled how, furthermore, "pride and show, and even waste, were flaunted in a new and still fairly virgin land—in the face of poverty and want not on the part of those who would not work, but the poverty and want of those who were all too eager to work, and almost on any terms." In the light of such facts he had come to believe that the case of Clyde

Griffiths was a typical result of the fierce competitive spirit. He now reaffirmed how not only typical but also approved by all the standard *mores* was Clyde's longing to rise.

In the novel itself he had made other generalizations about America. In dwelling upon Clyde's and Roberta's ignorant lack of preparation for life, he had observed how both their families in their unthinking narrow moralism were "excellent examples of that native type of Americanism which resists facts and reveres illusion." Incidentally, he introduced a new source to which such a boy and girl would turn for their standards of judgment and taste. Clyde, casting around for any means to escape Roberta, recalls a fake wedding he had seen in a movie. Roberta, looking forward to their marriage, is pathetically determined to have the same kind of taffeta afternoon dress that a screen heroine has worn.

In studying the lines of demarcation and stratification in Lycurgus, Dreiser is aware that they are hardly peculiar to America, but he wants to give his particular American facts to the full, and even notes—though it is not central to his purpose—how the native girls in the factory hold themselves aloof from the foreign-born. In his documentation of the trial he emphasizes how the question of Clyde's guilt or innocence becomes a mere incident in the struggle between rival politicians. The Republican District Attorney is also currently a candidate for Judge, so it is natural for Clyde's Democratic lawyers to oppose him by every means they can.

Many other such details could be cited. European observers were to comment upon the restlessness and uprootedness of Clyde's life in contrast to the more fixed patterns that still prevailed among them, as also upon the absence of any traditional culture even in the upper class. But Dreiser's central thought in putting the word American into his title was the overwhelming lure of money-values in our society, more nakedly apparent than in older and more complex social structures. And just as the flame was more bright and compelling, so were its victims drawn to it more helplessly.

But are such victims figures for tragedy? There has hardly ever been a more unheroic hero than Clyde, and Dreiser did everything he could not to build him up. He is good-looking, to be sure, with his black hair and white skin and nice smile, and with a wistfully appealing quality that makes him superficially attractive—indeed, not unlike a minor movie hero. But Dreiser keeps repeating that he is essentially selfish, with no steadily deep feelings for others, and with no serious consideration for Roberta in her trouble. Dreiser tells us near the beginning that Clyde, over-impressed by every sign of wealth, revealed "a soul that was not destined to grow up." As he moves into the final debate with himself over what to do about Roberta, his weak and scattered mind is never able to face the real facts. He shows no trace of greater maturity at this time of crisis.

As Clyde plots murder in spite of himself, Dreiser goes to the opposite extreme from the writer of a detective story. Everything that Clyde does is so inept that he is discovered at once. He plans nothing straight and leaves every kind of clue in his wake, even letters in the trunk at his rooming house that spell out the whole situation. These he had kept out of "an insane desire" for anything that showed "a kindness, a tenderness toward him." No wonder the prosecution regards him as possessing only "the most feeble and blundering incapacity." And he is hardly more than a puppet in his own attorneys' hands as he sits listening to the line of defense in which they coach him. They know that they can do nothing with the unlikely truth of the accidental killing without dressing it up. They present him as "a mental and moral coward," who underwent "a change of heart" towards Roberta, and decided to marry her after all. He recites this lie by rote. The charged hostility of the unbelieving courtroom is relieved by "the solemn vengeful voice" of a woodsman: "Why don't they kill the God-damned bastard and be done with him?"

Yet Dreiser does not mean us to share in this judgment, and we do not, despite the immense problem he faced in creating any sympathy for such a pawn. Earlier American writers had dealt with the theme of young men driven to murder by forces stronger than themselves, but their emphases had been very different. Hawthorne's Donatello, in boyish devotion to Miriam, acted in sudden unthinking frenzy to free her from the sinister figure who shadowed her. Melville's Billy Budd, horrified by the falseness of the accusation that he had been plotting mutiny, hit out instinctively, and (as Captain Vere said) it is as though Claggart were "struck dead by an angel of God." James's Hyacinth Robinson, caught between the conflicting claims of his devotion to the Princess Casamassima and the commands of the political underground to perform a revolutionary murder, cannot support the tension, and chooses suicide instead. In each case the study is one of essential innocence, and the weakness of a Hyacinth Robinson is not enough to interfere with our feeling for him.

But Dreiser had gone farther even than Melville in his questioning of free will. In presenting Clyde he gave the most complete illustration of his belief that "the essential tragedy of life" is that man is "a waif and an interloper in Nature," which desires only "to work through him," and that he has "no power to make his own way." He can lead us to respond to Clyde's situation only to the extent that we follow the defense attorney's description of him as "a mental and moral coward" into the further statement: "Not that I am condemning you for anything that you cannot help. After all, you didn't make yourself, did you?" This is the same expression Dreiser had used in *The Hand of the Potter*. One of Clyde's last fumbling reflections in the death house returns again to the essential point: "Would no one ever understand—or give him credit for his human—if all too human and perhaps wrong hungers—yet from which so many others—along with himself suffered?" Powys said of Dreiser: "No man I ever met is so sympathetic with weakness." A crucial element in our final estimate of this novel is how far he can enable us to participate in his compassion.

He has deprived himself of many of the most powerful attributes of traditional tragedy. Rejecting the nineteenth-century myth of the free individual, which his experience has proved to him to be false, he has now gone to the opposite pole in portraying an individual without any purposive will. He has decided that a situation like Clyde's was far more widely typical of America than one like Cowperwood's. But if in a sense Cowperwood was above tragedy, Clyde is below it, since there can be no real drama without conflict. In *Pierre* Melville had made his most devastating critique of optimistic individualism. But caught by his own despair he had also presented a young character so dominated by fate that we do not have the catharsis that can come only out of some mature struggle against doom.

Dreiser is not despairing in *An American Tragedy*. He is writing with objective detachment. But as is the case in most of O'Neill's plays, he sees man so exclusively as the overwhelmed victim that we feel hardly any of the crisis of moral guilt that is also at the heart of the tragic experience.

But in considering the final effect of the novel we must not fail to reckon with the several chapters after the trial. For here, as he deals with the long months of waiting in the brutal death house, he makes a detailed study of the religious appeals held out to Clyde by his mother and by a young evangelistic minister. Dreiser describes Mrs. Griffiths as "a figure out of the early Biblical days of her six-thousand-year-old world," and really conveys her as such in her square-shouldered if anguished trust in her son, even after his conviction, and in her unwavering if defeated effort to secure his pardon. It may come as more of a surprise that Dreiser speaks of the Reverend Mr. McMillan as a present-day Saint Bernard or Savonarola: "a strange, strong, tense, confused, merciful, and too, after his fashion beautiful soul; sorrowing with misery, yearning toward an impossible justice."

Here the qualifications that clog the prose are also a chief source of Dreiser's strength. To a greater extent even than in his earlier books he was determined to hold on with unrelaxed tenacity until he had given the full record, and he did not want his own unbelief to reduce his preacher to a satirized stereotype. The effect of the Reverend Mr. McMillan's efforts to bring consolation to Clyde is, to be sure, ironic. For as he gains the young man's confidence and hears his whole story, he comes to the saddened conclusion that, though Clyde may be technically innocent on legal grounds, his whole tangled train of thoughts and actions makes him deeply guilty in the eyes of God. But he does not turn against Clyde, but labors to bring him to contrition and conversion. He thinks that he has succeeded. But though Clyde, under his prompting, signs a statement to that effect, as he walks to the electric chair he is not at all sure that he really believes. Nor has there been any of the final recognition of his destiny that frees a Hamlet or a Raskolnikov. Clyde is still a cornered animal.

The street scene of the epilogue, paralleling that of the prologue, makes some small but important thematic additions. The father, who has played such a dim part in Clyde's life, looks even more ineffectual than before. The mother is still the one figure in the group who radiates a preserving if blind trust in divine providence, but her face is now "seamed with lines of misery." When her little grandson, "unsoiled and unspoiled and uncomprehending"—and paying no attention to the service—asks her for a dime to buy an ice-cream cone, she gives it to him thinking of Clyde, thinking that she must be "more liberal" with this boy, and not try to restrain him too much. But essentially she has learned nothing, and the whole course of events might easily be repeated. We feel "the vast scepticism and apathy of life" with greatly increased pressure. Dreiser has not shaped a tragedy in any of the traditional uses of the term, and yet he has written out of a profoundly tragic sense of man's fate. He has made us hear, with more and more cumulative power, the "disastrous beating" of the Furies' wings.

This distinction between tragedy and a tragic sense was not made by the reader who saw this novel most nearly with Dreiser's own eyes. Clarence Darrow read it with complete intensity, moved most by Dreiser's "fanatical devotion to truth," and he felt at the end that he had been "gripped in the hands" of such "a master of tragedy . . . as the world has seldom known." He also said: "Of course my philosophy is practically the same as yours." This kinship between Dreiser and Darrow may help us to define a little more thoroughly what it was that *An American Tragedy* brought to articulation out of our life, and what its significance is in the drift of our cultural history.

The philosophy that these two men shared had, of course, been Darrow's before it was Dreiser's. He was fourteen years the senior, also a product of the Middle West, where he likewise experienced poverty and inferior schooling. But his father was the village agnostic of Kinsman, Ohio, well read in Jefferson, Voltaire, and Paine. By the time therefore that Darrow managed to have a year in the Michigan Law School, his mind was already grounded in a firm rationalism such as Dreiser never knew. One of his major experiences was reading Altgeld's *Our Penal Code and Its Victims* (1884), with its compelling demonstration that the poor man does not receive equal justice. The connecting strand in all his various defenses that brought him to national prominence was his conviction that the criminal is not a free agent.

Darrow's final views, as expressed in *The Story of My Life* (1932), are extraordinarily akin to the burden of *An American Tragedy*. They bear out from a different angle why minds growing to maturity in the late nineteenth century felt such a break with earlier American tradition. Faced with the gross inequalities of Chicago financial life, Darrow came to doubt the doctrine of natural rights expressed by his father's eighteenth-century philosophers. He was to go much farther than that in casting off all traditional sanctions, and to regard any belief in a purposive universe as mere delusion. Like Dreiser he could only brood upon the "meaninglessness" of existence.

And yet, no matter how far-reaching his scepticism, like Dreiser he preserved a core of deeply humane values. His chief concern was the same as that in *An American Tragedy:* society's immense fallibility in arriving at justice. He considered crime as a sickness to be cured. When he developed his theory of how the cure might be effected, he again voiced some of Dreiser's most pervasive thoughts: "Most men and women are haunted by poverty, and all are helpless in the clutch of a relentless fate. . . . To prevent burglary the cause must be removed; it can never be done in any other way."

In regarding the victims of the law he too quoted the line about "the hand of the potter." His most condensed conclusion could have served as an epigraph for Dreiser's treatment of Clyde: "I have always felt sympathy for all living things. . . . I have judged none, and therefore condemned none. I believe that I have excused all who are forced to live awhile upon the earth. I am satisfied that they have done their best with what they had."

This close correspondence between the values of the two men makes us more aware of how representative these values are of their times, more aware too of why Dreiser held them. He viewed a society in which the equality whereon alone democratic justice might be based had been destroyed by the oligarchy of wealth. At this point he was not thinking in political terms; he entertained no ideas of how Clyde's world might be changed; he only contemplated it with somber resignation. Contemplating for ourselves the extreme to which both Darrow and Dreiser had gone in their scepticism, we are faced with the grave question of how long positive values can endure only as the aftershine of something that has been lost. Dreiser began to sense this as the 'twenties moved into the 'thirties, and he was caught up far more directly into political thinking than he had ever been before.

In the meantime *An American Tragedy* was his first immediate popular success, with a sale of twenty-five thousand in its initial six months, which still left it far below the ranks of a best seller. It was banned only in Boston. Mencken, who no longer needed to be Dreiser's champion, summed up the consensus of favorable opinion when he said: "Dreiser can feel, and, feeling, he can move. The others are very skillful with words." Wells agreed with Bennett that here was "one of the greatest novels of this century. It is a far more than life-size rendering of a poor little representative corner of American existence, lighted up by a flash of miserable tragedy. . . . It gets the large, harsh superficial truth that it has to tell with a force that no grammatical precision and no correctitude could attain." The word "superficial" is important to note, particularly as coming from a European. The shallowness of a Clyde prevents his history from ever reaching the transfiguration that Dostoevsky dwells upon in the closing pages of *Crime and Punishment*.

But the thoroughness of Dreiser's treatment, the realization we have at the end that his mind has moved inexhaustibly, relentlessly over every relevant detail raises the book to the stature that made Joseph Wood Krutch speak of it as "the great American novel of our generation." There were still many dissenting voices. Clyde's whole experience was too undifferentiated, too unilluminated to compel the attention of some readers already habituated to the masterpieces of the modern psychological novel. But for young men growing up in the 'twenties and 'thirties here was a basic account of the world to which they were exposed.

Dreiser's Politics

DREISER was now affluent for the first time in his writing career. After the moving-picture rights to *An American Tragedy* had been arranged, he moved into a duplex apartment on West 57th Street, and also bought a country place near Mt. Kisco overlooking Croton Lake. Bystanders began to note his new flashy clothes as he strolled down Broadway from the Ansonia twirling a slender cane or with a Russian wolfhound in leash. George Jean Nathan was amused by his "Caribbean blue shirts, vanilla ice-cream socks, and pea-green bow ties." It began to look as though his later years might run parallel to those of Arnold Bennett, as though with success he might accept the commercial world on its own terms.

But this appearance was deceptive inasmuch as the next work he turned to was the arrangement of a volume of his poems. He had been writing these off and on for a decade and thought of them as "lyrical philosophy." He said that he had found this mode of expression "out of a mystic despair." His conception of both his content and his form is indicated by his title *Moods Cadenced and Declaimed*. But his words were not exact enough to suggest a speaking voice, and even less than Sherwood Anderson did he have a control over free verse that could give its loose patterns any of the weight of his prose. This does not lessen the importance of these poems for Dreiser himself, as an instrument in keeping his spirit alive.

In the year after *An American Tragedy* he also wrote one of his most powerful short stories, "Typhoon," as a kind of companion piece. Here the deserted girl, Ida Zobel, threatens to kill her lover, and the pistol goes off inadvertently and does kill him. She is let off by the jury after her baby is born. But she cannot live with the fact that she brought about Ed's death—cruel and brutal though he had been in his refusal to marry her—so she drowns herself in King Lake Park, the scene of their first coming together. Dreiser's chief reason for so deliberately retracing old ground is voiced in some sentences near the end which declare how the world is too "busy, strident, indifferent, matter-of-fact" to pay heed to the inner meaning of tragedies. The other and somewhat less notable stories that he now collected in *Chains* also give point to this title in that they all illustrate some overpowering force, some love or hate or fear, inhibition, jealousy, or greed that has chained its protagonist to his fate.

With the leisure now to travel, Dreiser branched out into new interests and accepted the kind of invitation which the Soviet Union frequently gave in the nineteen-twenties through its Bureau of Cultural Relations, an invitation to visit Russia and see for himself what the country was doing. At the end of 1927 he spent three months there. Though he was very suspicious at first, he found that he could move around unhindered. The book he wrote about this experience, *Dreiser Looks at Russia,* is no more penetrating than those by other first visitors to a country of which they do not know the language; it is significant only in the light it casts on Dreiser himself.

Just the year before he made this trip he enunciated again what he had said so often, that he had "no theories" about "the solution of economic and political problems." The opening sentence of his book affirmed: "I am an incorrigible individualist—therefore opposed to Communism." He found many things in Russia to object to. He liked censorship there no better than at home, and noted wryly the tendency toward a smiling official version of life—which he said was what had prevented Stanislavski from producing Patrick Kearney's dramatization of *An American Tragedy*, the censors having declared it "too grim." In a chapter on "The Tyranny of Communism" he noted "the inescapable atmosphere of espionage and mental as well as social regulation which now pervades every part of that great land. The prying. The watching." And he made his severest criticism when he continued: "If one's offense or alleged offense chances to be political, or worse, anti-communistic—real hope of a fair and impartial trial is slight."

Like a number of other travelers at that time, however, Dreiser was deeply impressed by the release of so much hitherto untapped energy, by the confident belief he encountered on the part of many Russians that they could build a new world. It is not surprising that one thing he said he would "never forget" was "that via Communism, or this collective or paternalistic care of everybody—it is possible to remove the dreadful sense of social misery . . . which has so afflicted me in my own life in America and ever since I have been old enough to know what social misery was."

A book so divided in its judgments was destined to please nobody. Soviet critics saw in him the limitations of the bourgeois writer, but he got into worse trouble with the New York reporters on his return. With them he raised the question of why there should be breadlines in a country of America's resources, and added that on those grounds at least, "between the free and uncontrolled grafting we face here daily and a regulated accumulation centered in the Government, I prefer the Russian system."

Yet shortly after his return he was to write in "My City" a prose and verse celebration of New York for possessing, in spite of all its brutal contrasts, a compelling vitality beyond all the other cities of the world. A couple of years later he had changed his mind, had come to think of New York as "sinister," "a handsome woman with a cruel mouth." Conditions had become much worse, he said, than when he had pictured Hurstwood.

What had just intervened was the beginning of the long depression. Dreiser, having motored across the United States in the spring and early summer of 1930, entered at that time on a basic change in his views about the country and his own relation to it. Politics became a central interest for him, as it had not been before; and it was to continue so for the remaining fifteen years of his life. For this reason we should turn back to his earlier views and examine their evolution. The course of his political opinions was by no means always coherent, and it was often very unpopular. But these opinions are an integral part of his career, an integral part also of the recent American record; and it is important that they should be understood even by those who reject them.

He ultimately traveled a long distance from the views that had crystallized for him after his first reading of Spencer. Then, as we have seen, he believed that the doctrine of the Survival of the Fittest articulated the primary law of American behavior by making clear how the rich few had in the post-Civil War years shackled almost unbreakable controls over the many. In the light of that rapid and fierce development, he held that any effectual democracy was a lost dream, a part of the copy-book world he had been taught at school that did not square at all with the facts.

He took refuge at first in his own version of Spencer's theory of existence as an equilibrium between forces, "in a healthy swinging of the pendulum of life and time to and fro between the rich and the poor." But he could not persuade himself that the two sides were at all matched, and the disparity between them appeared to be widening. As a writer he could hold to the proposition that "without contrast there is no life," and he was always fascinated by this contrast as a dramatic spectacle. But as a citizen he began to feel more and more lost. In spite of all the talk about "the brotherhood of man and the freedom and independence of the individual," when he went through any of our big cities and saw the crippling of so many lives in the tenements and slums he could not accept any of the traditional slogans. He came to speak of "the profound delusion of equality under democracy," and virtually to mock at those who were innocent enough to believe in it. From here it was only a step to mocking at the mass itself for being so supine before its enslavers. From that step Dreiser was saved, as Mencken (say) was not, by his feeling of deep involvement with the poor from whom he had come.

But his education in political possibilities and responsibilities was very slow. We may recall that at the outset, as a young man eager to get on, he had been too much absorbed in the drama of individuals, with what he called "the poetry of life," to pay much attention to what he dismissed as "such minor things as politics." He was quite ready to grant in *Newspaper Days* that he had been completely self-centered: "I was ready to accept socialism if by that I could get what I wanted, while not ready to admit that all people were as deserving as I by any means."

This off-hand remark points up the fact that he had shown no active concern with the political radicalism that might have conditioned his youth. Though he had come out of Debs's Indiana, he seemed hardly aware of it; and, once he had moved on to New York, that awareness did not grow. After having been one of the submerged himself, he inclined during his editorial years to less exacting issues. When, for instance, the typographers' union worked for recognition at Butterick's, he was hardly more than luke-warm. In 1912 he revealed no more vital interest in the Progressives than he had taken earlier in the Populists—partly the result of his deep disillusionment over the possibility of their accomplishing anything. Beyond this, the creator of Cowperwood stated to an interviewer that he was "not a propagandist" in any cause. "Reform has a tendency to put all but the biggest temperaments in a cocksure intellectual attitude—and that attitude puts one terribly out of harmony with the great underlying life forces. The gods take their revenge on the cocksure." The degree of his distrust of reformers at this time was such as to make him even somewhat suspicious of Sandburg's poems because of the socialist attitudes behind them. During his years in Greenwich Village he was acquainted with Emma Goldman and Bill Haywood and Lincoln Steffens; but his own preoccupation remained with revolutionary ideas, not with revolutionary politics. Like many other intellectuals of the time he was opposed to our becoming involved in the European war, partly out of his deep-seated distrust of "the despicable British aristocracy," partly also out of a residue of truculent sympathy with his own native stock.

Only with the postwar period did he begin to demonstrate any active interest in national elections. In 1920 he wrote: "This fall, if I vote, I vote for Debs." His support was tentative, to be sure, on somewhat the same grounds that led him to vote for LaFollette four years later—his growing belief that the monopolists must be opposed. But he could still say: "I don't care a damn about the masses. It is the individual that concerns me."

During the remainder of the 'twenties he still shied away from commitment to any specific programs, out of his prevailing doubt whether, though many things were wrong with society, anything effective could be done to change them. But after his long trip across the country at the time of its economic collapse, he felt as though a new stage in his education had begun. He was soon to speak, as he had not previously done, of "the obligations of the individual to the organized society from which he derives." He also said, in the winter of 1931: "The time is ripe for American intellectuals to render some service to the American worker." He was actively engaging in the Tom Mooney case, as he had not done in that of Sacco and Vanzetti; but he commented now on the general indifference that had met the efforts to obtain a new trial for the Italian anarchists. As he set himself to writing *Tragic America,* a book of economic and social comment, he must have been aware of the widening of his title from *An American Tragedy.*

This period of re-education was also one of many personal difficulties. He had completed *Dawn*, at which he had worked off and on for years, and in going back again over his early career, up through his arrival in New York, he was struck by differences in the world that faced him now: "It's much worse to-day, and I ought to know. Then I was one of the starving myself, and yet I felt something adventurous and exciting about New York, about the whole country; if not for me, then for others luckier than me. There was a hope for individuals. To-day I have plenty to live on, and I see no hope anywhere."

Within a year his own margin of financial security would be wiped out by the failure of Liveright's firm. Even before that, he had quarreled bitterly with Liveright over the question of royalties on the moving picture of *An American Tragedy*. The making of this picture became a detailed illustration of how, as he now believed, the world of finance capital operated to crush human life. Lasky, who had bought the rights shortly after the novel's appearance, had then shied from presenting such a frank portrayal to the censored moving-picture public, and for some years had delayed doing anything about it. Then followed the episode of Eisenstein's rejected scenario—for which, as the Russian director said, Dreiser fought "like a gray-haired lion." The film finally completed in 1931 seemed to Dreiser, and to many other writers and critics to whom he appealed, to rob the story of any trace of "the inscrutable ways of life and chance," and to fail utterly to show how guilty society itself was; what was left was the shallowest kind of sex-murder film. Dreiser brought suit to prevent its being shown, even though he knew that he had no chance of succeeding.

His temper was at its most intransigent during that winter. When at a public dinner Sinclair Lewis accused him of having plagiarized from Dorothy Thompson's book on Russia, Dreiser slapped his face. Dreiser's version of the issue (which Miss Thompson has never contradicted) is that the two had been in the Soviet Union at the same time, talking to the same people and to each other, and reading many of the same Soviet pamphlets. But the real issue was lost sight of in the notoriety given to the slapping. As Dreiser approached his sixtieth birthday, instead of being honored by the press for his contribution to our letters, he was most often presented as a ludicrous grotesque.

His house at Mt. Kisco having burned down, he felt more uprooted and solitary than ever. Fortunately, his undiminished curiosity about what was happening in the world distracted him from his own problems. To gather material for his book he investigated conditions in Passaic and Paterson, and in the early summer he visited the mines in the Pittsburgh area. By then, as was the case with so many other Americans at the depth of the depression, his politics had gone through a rapid evolution. Though he joined no party he declared himself sympathetic with the general aims of communism, and agreed in particular with many of the views of William Z. Foster, another son of immigrants who had grown up in the midst of poverty; but he also declared that the main object of his exposure of conditions was to persuade America to take steps that would stave off revolution.

It should be remarked at once that Dreiser had no real gifts as a pamphleteer. The kind of documentation that served him well for the broad effects of fiction was too imprecise for detailed economic analysis, and betrayed him into many errors of fact. *Tragic America* had few favorable reviews, even on the left. The *New Masses* said that he failed to grasp the principles of Marxism; and Norman Thomas, believing him to be too much influenced by communist thought, said that the book was important only because a man of Dreiser's stature had written it. But Dreiser's leading ideas are not dependent upon the detailed mastery of his material, and they alone need concern us in our account of the evolution of his thought. He was still more indebted to Gustavus Myers than he was to Marx. When he had first read Myers he had drawn on him in his business novels for evidence of "the almost hopeless nature of democracy." He had paid little heed to the socialist faith that had motivated Myers's investigations into our rapacious capitalism. But now he was far closer to that position. He was also drawing on such conservative analyses as that made by the Wickersham Committee, appointed by President Hoover, which stated that America had by now "created the widest spread between the extremes of wealth and poverty existing in the whole world."

Many of the economic conditions pointed out by Dreiser in this book, which he first thought of calling *A New Deal for America*, were shortly to be tackled by the Roosevelt administration. But the basic fact that he had now learned was the destructiveness of that uncurbed individualism which had formerly fascinated him in a Cowperwood. The most crucial change in his thought was on the question of equality. At the time of *The Titan* he had summed up what had long been his dominant stand: "The idea that all men are created equal is one of the fundamental errors of our system of government." But now, seeking a description of himself as outside any party, he said he was "an Equitist." He had come to realize, as he had not done before, that the fundamental point was not that men differ widely in their abilities, but that they "should have equal *consideration,* not merely equal *rights,* before the law."

He was no longer willing to accept the theory that the present system was "the work of sheer fate." For this system seemed to be breaking down on every hand, and now at last he felt a renewal of faith in "the masses, from whom much good has already come and will come in the future." He was not at all sure that the American people, who had often struck him as apathetic, could be awakened to seize upon their precarious opportunity; but he had mastered the primary truth that there could be no real political freedom without the removal of our vast economic inequalities.

For the rest of his life Dreiser fought on every possible occasion to implement this truth. His first significant act was to accept in the spring of 1931 the chairmanship of the National Committee for the Defense of Political Prisoners, of which Lincoln Steffens was treasurer. The first case with which the Committee had to deal was that of the "Scottsboro boys." Shortly after finishing *Tragic America* he joined a group to investigate the terrorizing of the union organizers among the coal miners in Harlan County, Kentucky. It is hardly necessary to itemize here all the other causes with which he was connected. He was wrong-headed on many issues. He contradicted himself many times. As a speaker he was often angry, and sometimes given to overbearing tirades. Yet the main drift of his thought is unmistakable, and he took that thought with seriousness and responsibility.

The newspapers quite naturally played up how local Kentucky patriots had propped toothpicks against the door of Dreiser's hotel bedroom, and then—finding the next morning that these were still in place—declared that he had been sleeping with his secretary. What was read by far fewer people was "Individualism and the Jungle," the essay that grew out of his observing the operation of the mines. He was even firmer than before on "the immense injury which property in America" had continued to inflict upon labor, adding that the poor man had become more and more "an Ishmael in the land." He condensed (as he had not done before) his objections to the uncurbed individual who is free to. impose his rapacious will on others. He was ready now to urge on every hand the need to co-operate "for a better and more equitable order."

He pursued this goal by a course very much his own. In 1932 he voted for Foster, because "capitalism has failed as a system of government"; but he resigned from various committees when he decided that they were controlled by Communists, and said, "I am not an exact Marxian by any means." He also devoted a good deal of time to working for unity among the various groups on the left, knowing that otherwise they could only prove ineffectual. In 1934 he supported Upton Sinclair in his campaign for governor of California and praised him for recognizing fully "that the Capitalistic machine that got under way at the close of our idealistic Civil War" has "run its course and ended." Dreiser knew now beyond question that he was himself a Socialist, though he added: "Whether . . . Socialism in a modified form is ever permanently possible in America is another question. It is an ideal, and, as an ideal, enlists the enthusiastic support of millions, among whom I count myself one."

But he grew into a humane socialist philosophy largely through fighting within himself the most destructive prej-

udice of our time, anti-Semitism. It is typical of the truc-
ulence of Dreiser's thought that he got engaged at all in
a controversy on this explosive question: typical of his
dogged veracity that, once engaged, he did not attempt to
extricate himself by any smooth palliation of what he had
said.

The unfortunate starting point was an essay in *The
American Spectator*, of which sophisticated periodical Dreiser was an uneasy editor for a couple of years until his
resignation in 1934. This essay was cast as a conversation
among the editors—Nathan, Boyd, Cabell, O'Neill, and
Dreiser himself. It was Boyd who suggested that they
should discuss the Jews, and Dreiser led off with the proposition that "the world's quarrel with the Jew is not that he
is inferior, but that he is superior." He went on to cite the
enormous cultural contributions made by the Jews in the
two hundred years during which most of the bans against
them had been removed, whereas Nathan voiced a somewhat lower estimate of this contribution. The chief point
of the conversation—again advanced by Dreiser—was that
the Jews should establish a nation of their own.

The most offensive quality in the essay was its casualness
of tone at a time—1933—when Hitler's advent was making
anti-Semitism such a serious issue. Disturbed by this tone,
Hutchins Hapgood wrote Dreiser asking him to clear up his
position. In reply Dreiser revealed how deeply he had disliked the Jewish lawyers and businessmen with whom he
had had to deal in his frustrating battle with Hollywood.
He generalized from this experience, though casting his remarks objectively: "If you listen to Jews discuss Jews, you
will find that they are money-minded, very pagan, very
sharp in practice." He also cited a query by the Pennsyl-

vania Bar Association as to whether Jewish lawyers have "the fine integrity" endorsed by other lawyers. When in 1935 Hapgood printed this interchange, controversy raged.

A group from the *New Masses* who interviewed Dreiser were not at all satisfied. He seemed to take the whole matter too lightly, to rest upon: "I am an individual. I have a right to say what I please." Only slowly and "with the greatest hesitation" did he come to see more of the contradictions in his position, and to say: "Of course I make a distinction between the classes . . . between the Jewish worker and the Jewish exploiter. Everybody knows that I am anti-Capitalist. I identify the interests of the Jewish worker with the interests of all other workers. . . . I have no hatred for the Jew and nothing to do with Hitler or fascism." His interviewers still felt that he had a long way to go if he was to maintain his place "as a fighter for human liberty." The *Nation* hoped that he would see "the gross error of his ways," and not turn "traitor to intelligence" as Gerhart Hauptmann had done in Germany.

Dreiser followed the pack of intelligence, but, as in all matters, at his own gait. A year later he added: "I never said that as a race (in its entirety) I wholly disliked and distrusted them. I have paid my compliments to very, very many, and still do. . . . I admit that my attitude is in part emotional. I have said I have had a certain kind of typical experience with Jews, especially in practical matters, and of unvarying consistency. . . . At a time like this, when social unrest, nationalism, jingoism, etc. are so rampant, an attitude like mine might in some group, somewhere, lead to a pogrom, to social persecution of the very cruelest and bitterest nature. Yet this is decidedly what I do not want."

But not until 1939 had he purified his thought to the point of speaking out forthrightly against the "barbarism" of the Nazis, against "social torture of any group, or race, or sect for reasons of difference in appearance or creed or custom." To this he added that only collective action can ever stamp out "the inequities and iniquities"; his prejudice had at last yielded to the strength of his new devotion to equalitarianism. In 1944, in a special OWI broadcast directed toward the German people, Dreiser spoke of the "thousands upon thousands of helpless and often heroic Jews."

The gradual clarification of Dreiser's position affords another instance of his slow but impressive re-education as a man moving from his sixties into his seventies. It should already be apparent that he did not give much time to fiction during these years, though he wrote enough uncollected stories to make up another volume. These do not add a great deal to what he had already undertaken, though one or two deal with new aspects of poverty in the depression. Like Whitman in his old age, Dreiser was finding it harder and harder to complete a work. He had started tentatively again on *The Bulwark* when he was asked in the summer of 1938 to attend a peace conference in Paris, and to go to Spain in order that on his return he might help to rally public opinion for the Loyalists. It might be said that he had allowed himself to be distracted from his proper sphere; but he no longer felt that his primary obligation was to fiction. He was impelled to do whatever he could to cope with the issues of the immediate world.

He was caught up and overtaken by the speed of events, and his next book, *America Is Worth Saving* (1940), is an expression of views that did not prevail—the left wing's views on why the United States should not become involved in the war. In 1936 he had voted for Roosevelt, and after his return from Spain he had had a sympathetic exchange of letters with the President on what could be done for the relief of the sufferers in that country's civil war. But his admiration for Roosevelt as one of our few great presidents began to change as a consequence of Roosevelt's foreign policy. For what had never changed in Dreiser was his violent distrust of the British Empire. The book in which he tried to state his case is hardly more than compiled, ghost-written in part, the hurried work of a publicist dealing often in fulmination and harangue. Its only residue of value is the passages revealing his further re-education in the potentialities of American democracy. He speaks of himself now as a revolutionary, fighting against the continued disproportion between wealth and poverty, but as a revolutionary with an American vocabulary. Looking back over our history he affirms that we have what we need in "those marvellous national documents of ours," the Declaration of Independence and the Constitution; that the revolution of our time is to implement these more effectively in economic and not merely political terms. When he declares that "the good is social good," he cites as witnesses Whitman, Henry George, and Bellamy.

In spite of all the severe tensions of our life, of all the things that were wrong with America, Dreiser can assure himself that "there is still so much that is right, that there lives on in the American people a spirit which is separate from and greater than any of the official acts and statements of America," a spirit that is resilient, independent, and yet kindly, with a saving salt of humor and scepticism. This formulation is a reminder that Dreiser was not always grim. He had written in 1937 an essay called "Democracy of the

Funnybone" in which he said that our attitude that "no one is sacred," that everything can be laughed at, was one of our strongest bulwarks against dictators. This was the Dreiser who was a longtime admirer of Mack Sennett, and a friend, in his later years, of Charlie Chaplin.

With the German attack upon Russia, Dreiser's attitude towards the war changed. In a conversation with Dos Passos in 1938 about the Soviet Union he had said: "I have begun to think that maybe it won't be any better than anything else." But in the light of the Russians' defense against Nazi Germany he knew that he stood with them, in a way that his blind hatred of the British Empire had prevented him from standing with the English. In spite of all the limitations and shortcomings of the Soviet Union, he still believed that "the dawn is in the East." It is hardly necessary to add at this point that he had no very close knowledge of Soviet politics, that he was on much solider ground, say, in his tribute to Gorki as one "incapable of compromise with his deepest feelings, tremendously moved by what he saw in life. The grandeur of his temperament made him the artist and revolutionary he was."

Many of the words of this tribute might be applied to Dreiser himself. Without Gorki's gift for language, his basic theme had been similar: the terrible privations of poverty —though the circumstances of Gorki's early life as one of the dispossessed in Czarist Russia were far more brutal than anything that Dreiser had experienced.

Few words of tribute came Dreiser's way at the time of his seventieth birthday in 1941, and even after our entry into the war his radical stand was still not popular. But he felt at this time a renewed closeness with old friends like John Cowper Powys and Edgar Lee Masters. As Powys put it in a letter to Masters: "You and D, we three who are closer than lovers with exactly the same amount of reverence and affection." Art Young, whose political battles in *The Masses* had antedated Dreiser's by many years, declared a strong sense of solidarity with him. He began to be warmly interested also in several younger writers, particularly Farrell, Odets, Steinbeck, and Richard Wright.

As the war went on, he felt less compulsion to engage in political activity and was often appalled by the endless bloodshed. He tried now to resume his fiction, but found his creative energies depleted, and was for several months in a state of serious depression. The future did not look at all clear, and he was not sure whether civilization might not go under. Yet when Mencken wrote him with his accustomed jauntiness in the spring of 1943: "What precisely are your ideas about the current crusade to save humanity?" he experienced a resurgence of conviction as he answered: "I do not know what can save humanity, unless it is the amazing Creative force which has brought 'humanity' along with its entire environment into being." As he continued, his mind went back over earlier stages of his career: "I, myself, have *cursed life* and gone down to the East River from a $1.50 a week room in Brooklyn to quit. My pride and anger would not let me continue, as I thought . . .

"You see, Mencken, unlike yourself I am biased. I was born poor. For a time, in November and December, once, I went without shoes. I saw my beloved mother suffer from want—even worry and wring her hands in misery. And for that reason, perhaps—let it be what it will—I, regardless of whom or what, am for a social system that can and will do better than that for its members—those who try, however humbly—and more, *wish to learn how* to help themselves, but are none-the-less defeated by the trickeries" of those "who believe that money . . . distinguishes them above all others."

This brings us back to the central issue that motivated Dreiser's politics. In the feverish period leading up to the war he often seemed only to be echoing the Communist position without adequate investigation of his own, often seemed very close to one of the worst danger points of our time—an unqualified acceptance of mass force for the good it can theoretically do. He moved away from this danger point as his meditations on the nature of equality deepened, as he realized that equality meant the equality of individuals co-operating to create the only effective freedom. He would no longer say that he was for either the individual or the mass. His belief continued to grow that a society which would do justice to both could be built only through socialism. In a letter to Madame Chiang Kai-shek in the summer of 1944, urging Chinese co-operation with the Soviet Union as well as with the United States, he said: "While America may appear to be the one glamorous, victorious and free country to the other nations of the world, we, here, stand in danger every moment of our lives of being completely dominated financially by the Capitalistic few at the top—about 5 %—who, even now, control 95% of the wealth. The only thing that keeps us seemingly progressive is the fact that we fight these monopolistic powers, or try to. . . . The progressive forces of the world are the ascending forces. And the ascending forces of the world are made up of the common man."

At this same time he recorded his radio broadcast to the German people, in which he spoke as the son of a German immigrant, and, after urging the need of "economic justice" in the postwar world, concluded with a plea for a renewed effort toward establishing "the Brotherhood of Man."

Our problem in evaluating all such utterances is the same as has confronted us throughout Dreiser's writing—the extent to which his standard terms still give expression to a depth of personal feeling. There is evidence from Dreiser's life at this time that he had achieved more inner serenity than he had previously known. During this summer and the following winter he felt an access of creative energy once more, and at last finished *The Bulwark* and turned again to *The Stoic*. In the summer of 1945, as the war was drawing to its close, he was more and more responsive to the principles of co-operation which Wendell Willkie had enunciated in *One World*. He was deeply stirred also by the way in which European writers and artists—Picasso and Sean O'Casey among them—were affirming their adherence to international solidarity by the symbolic act of joining the Communist Party.

We shall not be able to grasp all the reasons why Dreiser took the same step until we have looked more fully at the development of his later philosophy, at how much he now implied when he spoke, as in his letter to Mencken, of "the Creative force." At this point it is enough to note that when he said "the dawn is in the East" he was thinking not only of Russia, but of China and India, of the profound spiritual resources of the Orient. He was more religious than he had ever been before, and he may therefore have considered it necessary to assure his associates on the left that this did not involve any defection from them. The fact that Foster, for whom Dreiser had warm admiration, had again become head of the American Communist Party doubtless helped crystallize his decision. In any case he believed that the claims of both the self and the unself were justified in this act. He insisted that he would continue to speak his mind as he saw fit; that if the party did not approve it could expel him.

In judging his act we must remember the temper of the period in which it was made. His major concern was the prevention of further wars, which he was convinced would destroy civilization. He had slowly learned the lesson that there could be no humane life in the United States until the inequities should be removed that had thwarted or destroyed so many of the characters in his fiction. He now believed that the next step was to do everything he could to break down the destructive barriers of nationalism, and to work for equity among all the peoples of the world. Otherwise there would be no world in which to live.

Dreiser's Philosophy

TWO of Dreiser's most frequently quoted statements drive home the point that he had no fixed philosophy. He made the first of these at the beginning of *A Traveler at Forty:* "For myself, I accept now no creeds. I do not know what truth it, what beauty is, what love is, what hope is. I do not believe anyone absolutely and I do not doubt anyone absolutely. I think people are both evil and well-intentioned." The second, in 1928, was in answer to a request for his Credo. Here he began: "I can make no comment on my work or my life that holds either interest or import for me." His last two sentences carry the gist of what he had to say: "As I see him the utterly infinitesimal individual weaves among the mysteries a floss-like and wholly meaningless course—if course it be. In short I catch no meaning from all I have seen, and pass quite as I came, confused and dismayed."

In the light of such passages it would be idle to speak of Dreiser as a naturalistic novelist in the sense of having a system of human behavior that he wished to illustrate, just as we have already found it beside the point to speak of the development of his fiction in relation to the deliberate mechanical devices of Zola, of which he was mainly ignorant. Yet there is a wider and looser, but still authentic, sense in which he was a naturalist. From first to last he was driven to try to understand man's place in nature, to a far more profound degree than any of his American contemporaries in fiction; indeed, for a parallel we should have to go back to Melville's grapplings. This is what gave Dreiser's books their peculiar breadth: they are universal, not in their range of human experience, but in the sense that an only partly known universe presses upon and dominates his searching consciousness of what happens to all his characters.

Our main concern with the various stages in the development of his thought is not with its intrinsic value, but with the light it casts back upon his earlier fiction and forward upon *The Bulwark*. But Dreiser himself engaged in this thought with the greatest seriousness, and it therefore also becomes an essential part of any full image of him.

His persistent curiosity about science took the form, in his later years, of long summer visits to the biological laboratories at Woods Hole (in 1928) or at Cold Spring Harbor (in 1937), where he talked to the scientists and followed some of the experiments, as he also did at various New York medical schools. In California, where he settled permanently in 1938, he made contact with physicists and astronomers. He started these varied pursuits with the conviction that "the more we know, *exactly*, about the chemic and biologic and social complexities by which we find ourselves generated, regulated, and ended, the better."

One of the strongest scientific influences upon him, which had begun, indeed, when he was working on *The Financier*, was Jacques Loeb's *The Mechanistic Conception of Life*. Loeb's explanation of human instincts and behavior in physiochemical terms seemed to Dreiser the next natural step after Spencer and Darwin and Haeckel, and his own descriptions of love in terms of "chemisms" derive from this source. Yet Dreiser was never a consistent mechanist. Paul Elmer More, reviewing *Hey-rub-a-dub-dub* with the cool distaste of the new humanist, declared the distinguishing feature of these essays to be an "oscillation between a theory of evolution which sees no progress save the survival of the rapaciously strong and a humanitarian feeling of solidarity with the masses who are exploited in the process." This is a particularly interesting formulation in view of Dreiser's later development. At this point he had depicted his strongest hero, but not his weakest one. And as we have seen, it was several years after his depiction of Clyde that Dreiser advanced from his earlier feeling of pity for the helpless poor to his militant belief that their condition could be changed by mass action.

We have already observed how the sense of life that we feel in Dreiser's novels is larger and deeper than are any of the patterns of thought that they advance. Eliseo Vivas has argued that the very inconsistency in Dreiser's mechanism was what allowed this largeness to break through. Mechanism holds that life has no transcendent meaning that we can discover; but Dreiser, though he thought he accepted this, could not accept it with any equanimity. Hence, as Vivas argues, "his perplexity, his sense of futility," his harping on "the vanity of effort" in such a hopeless world. But his perplexity is due equally to the fact that he keeps searching for a transcendent meaning. He never really adhered to the pitiless implications of the Darwinian universe. As he admired the strong and sympathized with the weak, he became deeply involved with both. As he kept groping to find more significance in their lives than any his mind could discover, he dwelt on the mystery of the inexplicable as no rigorous mechanist would have done.

We can observe this same ambivalence in his approach to science. He expressed great reverence for the selfless pursuit of knowledge as he watched it at various laboratories. He argued against Sherwood Anderson's distrust of science as menacing the imaginations and emotions: "I think the reason people reject it is because they haven't got the capacity to see how enormously rich, mysterious, varied, and in fact, entirely satisfactory in an emotional way, science as such can be, while at the same time they are taking advantage of it in practical life." But he always became impatient with scientists who would not grant that "mystery" was part of "reality." The main drive of his interest was to pass beyond phenomena to their cosmic significance.

The most recurrent writing of the last decade of his life, which finally absorbed far more of his attention than his political pamphleteering, grew out of this interest. He finished several essays and projected several others for a volume that he thought of calling *The Formulae Called Life*. He undertook most of these when a long period of nervous ill health in 1934 and 1935 had plunged him into melancholy and morbid fears. As he emerged from this crisis he experienced a renewed influx of vitality. He felt once again that he could prize "the jewel which is the mind" even in the midst of loneliness.

The position that his essays developed took its start in what he had said as far back as *A Hoosier Holiday:* "I once believed," he wrote there, "that nature was a blind, stumbling force or combination of forces which knew not what or whither. . . . Of later years I have inclined to think just the reverse, i.e. that nature is merely dark to us because of her tremendous subtlety and our own very limited powers of comprehension."

He now considered that he had extended his powers at least a little way, and what he comprehended was quite different from the crass materialism that had once seemed the only law of life he could discern. In "The Myth of Individuality" (1934) he developed the proposition that "It is not the man that is living, but the race or races and their creative chemisms. Man is not living, but is being lived by something which needs not only him but billions like him in order to express itself." What distinguishes this proposition from his earlier recurrent thought that man does not use life, but is used by it, is its new grounding. For he now said explicitly that he was against all "mechanism," and began in subsequent essays to talk in terms of the "totality," which "we variously refer to as the Universe, God, or the Vital Force." If nature was still a "oneness" from which man had no separate will, this "oneness" was now a "universal mind." To illustrate his new reverence before this conception of nature, he quoted Emerson's "Brahma."

One may well ask how Dreiser squared this increasingly mystical thought with his concurrently developing interest in radical politics. Once again the comparison with Whitman is the most suggestive. Both of them, as they grew older, felt their strongest impulse towards a grasp of the universe in its wholeness. Neither had the formal training that would have raised barriers of logic against the syntheses that they felt bound to make between discordant realms. Whitman, no less than Dreiser, was occupied with the new discoveries of science while equally determined to pass beyond the limitations of science. And as he dwelt upon cosmic wholeness, he also dwelt more and more upon the need of solidarity in society, and his political thought —again like Dreiser's—moved from individualism towards socialism.

The only kind of coherence that one can find in such diverse and apparently contradictory pursuits is in the unity of personality behind them. In Dreiser's case we are confronted by the paradox that at the very time when he was denying the concept of the separable individual, in either the cosmos or the state, he was also drawn, as he had not previously been, to our earlier American transcendental thinkers. He immersed himself in Thoreau, and wrote a long introduction to a volume of Thoreau selections entitled *Living Thoughts* (1939). What delighted Dreiser most in this naturalistic philosopher was his fusion of science and intuition. He kept stressing Thoreau's insistence that "Man is related to all of Nature," that in Nature lies the source of all his knowledge; yet he confessed himself most moved by how Thoreau conveys the effect "of tapping" an "unconquerably limitless universe," by how he finally establishes Nature as "all mind." Dreiser added that of all the philosophers he had read in recent years, "from Democritus to Einstein," he had found Thoreau "most illuminative of the implications of scientific result" because of his staunch unwillingness to stop short with mechanical processes, because of his belief in "a universal and apparently beneficent control . . . however dark and savage its results or expressions may seem to us at times."

The fact that Dreiser discovered kinship with such a highly individualistic philosopher fills out the bases of his political beliefs in a way that his hurried pamphleteering often failed to do. He had arrived at the conviction that man cannot find fulfillment except through society. But he had not lost the individual in the mass; he still held to the conviction that it is the function of a good society to give release to every member's creative potentialities.

The fusion that Dreiser made between his observations of scientific order and his increasingly religious philosophy may be illustrated by an experience he reported to his old friend Marguerite Tjader Harris: "You know, that summer I was down at Cold Spring Harbor—one afternoon, after I'd been working all day in the laboratory, I came out in the sunshine and saw a little bunch of yellow flowers growing along the border of the park. I stooped over them. Here was the same beautiful design and the lavish, exquisite detail that I had been seeing all day through the microscope. Suddenly it was plain to me that there must be a divine, creative Intelligence behind all this. It was after that, that I began to feel differently about the universe. I saw not only the intelligence, but the love and care that goes into all created things."

This was the theme of one of his many unpublished essays, "My Creator" (1943), which was meant to form the conclusion to his book. Here he dwelt on the "design" that he now saw everywhere, in the avocado tree in his garden or in the farthest courses of the stars. He declared that he was "moved not only to awe but reverence" for the inevitable Creator of such divine and yet harmonious patterns, for the Creator too of "the intricate and interesting, and yet often enough, trying, and worse, terrible and yet not wholly unbeautiful structure . . . which we call life."

In the estimation of John Cowper Powys, essays like

these carried Dreiser below the "massive Balzacian" surfaces of his fiction to a spiritual reality that had been latent, if inscrutable, in him from the start. We can now perceive more clearly why when Dreiser said, "The dawn is in the East," he was mindful also of Indian thought, as Emerson, Thoreau, and Whitman also had been. All these earlier men, parched by the aridities of our formal theology, had regarded the Orient as a basic source of renewal. Dreiser, who as a result of his conditioning was far more hostile to the church than was any of the three, was at the end open to conviction, sympathetic with all genuine belief, if no systematic believer himself.

It was in this state of mind that, after many delays and distractions, he at last completed *The Bulwark*. This is a different kind of novel from any that Dreiser had done before. It does not have his usual documentation, his thorough if heavy immersion in material details. It reads more like a chronicle, the annals of Solon Barnes's family from his birth to his death. Part of the reason for this change lies in the thirty years' lapse between the book's inception and its completion. In his final draft Dreiser depended greatly upon Mrs. Harris to help him cut away all but the essentials of his theme. But another part of the reason is the theme itself, Solon Barnes being a Quaker who is very conscious of the divergence between his ways and those of the modern world. Incidentally, the long delay in the book's composition betrayed Dreiser into some inconsistencies in chronology. He had originally described Solon as coming of age in the eighteen-seventies, but in the final version he changed this to "take in the nineteenth century." As a result of this change Solon's younger children grow up in the nineteen-twenties. But there has been no mention of the

First World War; while the dancing of the "two-step" and the reference to automobiles as the exclusive possession of the rich betray the milieu as still that of the pre-war world.

To some readers Dreiser's style here has appeared plain to the point of thinness. Yet, as though in response to his material, he wrote with greater simplicity and spareness, with fewer broken-backed sentences than usual. We can judge the effect of the whole only if we realize that it is far more a symbolical than a naturalistic novel, basically as bare as a parable. Dreiser's favorite symbol of clothes is particularly effective here, the traditional Quaker dress being one of the chief factors that divide the Barnes family off from the luxury which the younger members begin to long for. Their late-eighteenth-century house is a symbol of ordered, spacious life; yet it is too elaborate for the stricter Quakers and too staid for the children. The clear stream flowing beside it becomes a recurrent embodiment of the love that Solon avows to Benecia along its bank until it becomes a symbol of separation years later after her death.

But a more detailed treatment of the operation of this and other symbols will come more appropriately after we have discerned the full meaning of the controlling symbol in the title. Solon is the bulwark, standing firmly for the older values in a changing world. His career is in Philadelphia banking, but his aims are as different as possible from Cowperwood's. He believes that a businessman should be a steward under the Lord, and he regards the depositors' funds as a sacred trust. Dreiser remarks that as treasurer Solon would not be one "who would eventually dream out a vast . . . street railway system"; he preferred the realm of smaller profits where "the troubled fare of ethics was not so plainly visible." Yet he was inevitably surrounded by promoters resembling Cowperwood, and the bank moved into speculative operations, into the era of giant corporations, despite his opposition. The irony that Dreiser originally conceived in his title begins to emerge.

It becomes far more sharply edged as Dreiser follows the relations of Solon with his five children. He is "the serious dignified father," cautious, humorless, a little dull. The atmosphere surrounding him and his wife has become too fixed and still "for frail, restless, hungry human need." The eldest daughter, Isobel, is aware of the widening gulf between their conservative home and "the expanding ideas" of the times, is aware too that she is plain, and becomes studious and lonely. The next boy and girl make their adjustments with the times. Their Quakerism is all on the surface: Orville knows how to combine decorous behavior with a solid bank account, and Dorothea marries the son of one of the new financial magnates.

The two youngest, Etta and Stewart, are of the sort whom Dreiser has always treated with greatest sympathy, and their tensions with their father form most of the novel's second half. These passages also resume leading themes from Dreiser's earlier work. Etta is lured by the "romance" of life; "slowly rocking in her little rocking chair," she dreams like Carrie of "color, motion, beauty." When she has just finished boarding school, her father discovers her reading Daudet's *Sapho;* her response to his denunciation is to leave home and join a school friend at the University of Wisconsin, and to refuse to come back. As she says in her own defense, "We simply want to know about life."

Since she is past eighteen, her father cannot withhold from her a family legacy, and when she and her friend move east to an apartment in Greenwich Village, the atmosphere resembles that of *The "Genius."* But since Dreiser makes no effort to cast an aura of glamour over Etta, her outlines remain distinct and real. She falls in love with a painter, who though he cares for her comes to feel that he must be free for the sake of his work; and what Dreiser dwells on is the pathos of the situation for Etta, since, despite her revolt, her realm "was really that of love and marriage." It is just when she feels utterly alone that her brother Stewart's tragedy occurs.

In many ways Stewart is like Clyde, though in his conflict the opposing sides are reversed: here the son of a well-to-do family reaches out avidly for pleasures that his father cannot comprehend. Stewart quickly decides that the Quaker teachings have "nothing to do with real life." Solon, berating him severely for attending a burlesque show, refuses to add to his small allowance, and Stewart begins stealing from his father's purse in order to go on week-end rides with the boys at school. Here Dreiser drew upon a New Jersey case he had read about in the papers. One of the working-class girls that the boys pick up dies of a heart ailment, and after the boys are arrested Stewart, overcome by adolescent shame and panic, kills himself.

The other bank officers had regarded Solon as a bulwark in a special sense—as someone whose respectability they particularly needed "to hide behind" in their new manipulations; and now he must resign. Yet the scene in which this happens lacks the irony it may have had in Dreiser's early plans for the book; for Solon has already begun to make a whole series of new discoveries that constitute a significant reversal of his—and Dreiser's—direction. Shocked out of his complacency by Stewart's tragedy, he has brooded on the state into which he himself has drifted. His renewed distrust of luxury has brought to the surface his latent doubts about his bank associates. When he goes to resign, therefore, it is not in response to the disgrace that has come on his family, but in order to denounce his associates' mushroom development of holding companies and to say that he wants no further part in this acquisitive society. His indictment elicits from the other directors no comment except that his principles are "too high for these days."

But Solon goes farther than this. After his wife's death from a stroke, he arrives at a reaffirmation of his faith. Dreiser makes a comprehending study of this renewal in a way that would hardly have been possible in his earlier fiction, but which we have been prepared for as we have followed the developing trends in his thinking. He could still denounce the Catholic Church for promoting "mass stupidity"; but as early as 1927 he had spoken of the teachings of Elias Hicks as "the most reasonable of all religions." The choice of Hicks—who, incidentally, was the strongest influence upon Whitman—was significant in that his emphasis, even beyond that of other Quakers, was upon the inner light and against the need of the outward marks of authority. It is equally significant that as Dreiser began to think in terms of the development of a more organic society, he said to Dos Passos in 1938 that the kind of community he wanted in America would have something like the Quaker conception of "spiritual relationship."

He drew upon his own experience, also, in some of the scenes portraying Solon's transformation. Walking beside the peaceful stream near which he had courted his wife long ago, Solon is reminded of the anguish of his loss until his attention is caught by a vivid emerald fly feeding upon and destroying a tiny bud—an example of the survival of the fitter at the expense of the less fit such as had taught Cowperwood the law of life in the battle he watched between the lobster and the squid. But Solon's reaction is very different: he is so enthralled by the beauty of the fly that, like Dreiser confronted with the flowers outside the biological laboratory, he is moved rather to an acceptance of natural order, of a cosmic if unfathomable purpose. Though unable to answer the question of why one should live and another die, he reflects: "Surely there must be a Creative Divinity, and so a purpose, behind all of this variety and beauty and tragedy of life. For see how tragedy had descended upon him, and still he had faith, and would have."

Even closer to an experience that Dreiser reported about himself was Solon's encounter with a puff adder. In 1938 Dreiser had come across one in the New York countryside and, thinking it poisonous, had killed it, only to learn that it was harmless, and to be sorry. The next time one crossed his path, he spoke to it, assuring it that he intended it no hurt, and had a sensation as though it understood. This anecdote (without the initial killing) is transferred to Solon, who finds in the experience another sign of the universal harmony of nature.

But Solon's chief meditations are grounded on something far solider than such elusive pantheism. From the surface of conventional observances he has found his way back to the core of the teachings of John Woolman, firmest of American Quaker radicals. As Dreiser weaves crucial passages from Woolman's *Journal* into his text, it is evident how much he had also meditated upon these. Woolman had not insisted that everybody else must join the Quaker sect; he did insist on human brotherhood in its simplest and most revolutionary form, on the freeing of all slaves, on economic equality. He is the natural apostle for Solon's belated rediscovery of Christian love, for the Solon who murmurs on his deathbed: "The banks, the banks . . . the poor and the banks."

But Solon's is not the last word in this parable. Etta, who has come home again after Stewart's death, has been united in forgiveness with her father, who finds himself close to her as he is not to his two respectable and successful children. As she reads aloud to him from his Quaker books, she also grasps for the first time in her life "the weight of spiritual beauty." But the novel ends on the day of her father's funeral. Orville encounters her crying beside their father's coffin, and is surprised that she should care, since, in his cool prudential eyes, she was the one responsible for starting all the family's troubles. She does not bother to get angry at him, but answers simply: "Oh, I am not crying for myself, or for Father—I am crying for *life.*"

This sentence is a final summation of what has been Dreiser's principal theme in all his most moving work. He felt it to be the natural coda to the book in which he had for the first time made a sympathetic study of the father image, of its transformation from austerity to loving tenderness. Dreiser seems also to have been aware that his creation of Solon involved in a sense a personal act of forgiveness, since he spoke of dedicating this novel to his own father's memory. The central truth that he wanted to affirm through Solon was that living authority lies not in the harsh judging mind but in the purified and renewed affections of the heart.

The book in which Dreiser tried to affirm these values has

been judged variously even in the few years since its appearance shortly after his death. By those sophisticates who hold that any return to religion is a mere "failure of nerve" it will doubtless continue to be dismissed as a piece of specious religiosity. However, that the values were real for Dreïser himself cannot be the line of defense against this charge, since in order to move a reader they must be embodied in the work itself. Dreiser's interest in the *Bhagavad Gita*, as we can now see, was also heartfelt, but he could not convey it through the unlikely channel of the closing pages of his Cowperwood trilogy. *The Bulwark* is very bare, many of its pages are blocked out rather than written, and it will hardly hold a place with *Sister Carrie* or *An American Tragedy*. But it is moving as an authentic if belated primitive, even farther away from the current modes of fiction than he himself had been at the beginning of his career. Like the self-taught painter, Dreiser had found an adequately functional form for what he had to express. Like Melville in the forty years from *Moby Dick* and *Pierre* to *Billy Budd*, he had progressed from a bitter questioning of the universe to a more serene acceptance—and yet his deepest burden was still compassion over all that remained inscrutable.

The months during which Dreiser was writing *The Bulwark* seem to have been one of the happiest periods of his life, one in which he felt a harmony between his inner and his outer worlds. His openness now to religious experience led him on several occasions to different churches, and on Good Friday, 1945, just as he was finishing *The Bulwark*, he partook of the Congregational communion service. It was after a short vacation that spring that he set himself to complete *The Stoic*, with the feeling that he had little time left.

Thought from *The Bulwark* overflowed into several of his last pieces of writing; and a poem, "What to Do," and an essay, "Interdependence," helped to establish finally the fusion he had achieved between his politics and his philosophy. He was thinking of Tolstoy as he wrote the poem, and its central images embody in the simplest form the chief sources to which he now turned for the bulwarks of the future:

"A small-town editor writes the truth about profit and starvation.

And one knocks at a broken door and when it opens hands in a loaf of bread.

And one, step by step, all day long, walks to this laborer and that saying united we stand, divided we fall.

And one, the workers' friend, says Vote, Speak, for you are the Government, By you your leaders rise or fall.

And one, the educator, says to the child, A.B.C. and to the adult, Learn! Know that the world grows smaller!

And one, the minister, says to all, Love thy neighbor as thyself.

And one, the lover of his fellow man, says Take, from each according to his ability; Give, to each according to his need."

That these images are familiar to the point of being stock would not have bothered Dreiser, any more than it would have bothered the later Tolstoy. They serve to demonstrate the double sources of his radicalism, in both economic and spiritual values. In the same month that he made his symbolic act of joining the Communist Party he declared: "The true religion is in Matthew."

One might simply say that he was an old man, untroubled by inconsistencies that subsequent events would have made obvious. But this is not really the main point. For he had found—if more essentially in Woolman than in Marx—beliefs that he was convinced the world could no longer afford to ignore. In the month after the end of the Second World War he said: "Only the mass can get the world out of its present mess. Interdependence, a new understanding between peoples all over the world is needed! But how are we to get that? First, the need is so great and the danger of the destruction of civilization so apparent and so close at hand, that men everywhere have begun to think of ways and means of surviving through contact and understanding of one another. . . .

"But," he went on, "when I speak of the mass I speak of the individuals of which the mass is made up. As soon as one begins to think of the other side as a mass or a crowd, the human link seems to go. We forget that crowds consist of individuals, of men and women, and children, who love and hate and suffer." It was there he took his stand, as he had throughout his fiction. The chief purpose of "Interdependence" was to urge the widest possible interchange between peoples in order to avert a recrudescence of that nationalism which he could now regard only as a virulent disease. The fact that the next years were to belie his hopes would not have shaken his conclusions: "To know and to understand is to love, not to hate."

On December 27, 1945, Dreiser was suddenly stricken with an attack in the kidneys, and died the next day. His funeral was conducted by Allen Hunter, the Congregational minister whom he had recently met, but John Howard Lawson also paid a tribute to Dreiser's social conscience, and Chaplin read one of Dreiser's own poems, "The Road I Came," on the mystery of the creative force. His will provided that, after Helen's death, whatever little property might be left should go to a home for Negro orphans.

Bibliographical Notes

The Editors are grateful to Mr. Robert Elias and Mr. Eugenio Villicaña for their help in the preparation of the bibliography.

BIBLIOGRAPHY

A Bibliography of the Writings of Theodore Dreiser, by Edward D. McDonald, Centaur Book Shop, Philadelphia, 1928, is an early listing of the novelist's works. *Dreiserana: A Book About His Books*, by Vrest Orton, Chocorua Bibliographies, New York, 1929, gives errata and addenda. *A Preliminary Checklist of Books and Articles on Theodore Dreiser*, by Ralph N. Miller, Western Michigan College Library, Kalamazoo, 1947, is at present the best critical listing of Dreiser criticism between 1912 and 1947. A briefer and more accessible bibliography is to be found in the third volume of the *Literary History of the United States*, Macmillan, New York, 1948.

WORKS

There is no collected edition of Dreiser's work. The order of his separate works and their reprints is as follows: *Sister*

Carrie (1900), B. W. Dodge, N. Y., 1907; Boni & Liveright, N. Y., 1917 (Modern Library reprint, 1931, with a new preface by the author). *Jennie Gerhardt* (Harper & Brothers, N. Y. and London, 1911): Garden City, N. Y., 1934 (Star Books). *The Financier* (Harper, N. Y., 1912): Boni & Liveright, N. Y., 1927, rev. ed.; Constable, London, 1931; World Publishing Co., Cleveland, Ohio, 1946. *A Traveler at Forty* (The Century Co., 1913). *The Titan* (John Lane, N. Y., 1914): Boni & Liveright, N. Y., 1925; Constable, London, 1929; Garden City, N. Y., 1935 (Star Books); World Publishing Co., Cleveland, Ohio, 1946. *The "Genius"* (John Lane, N. Y., 1915): Boni & Liveright, N. Y., 1927; Garden City, N. Y., 1935 (Star Books); World Publishing Co., Cleveland, Ohio, 1946. *Plays of the Natural and Supernatural* (John Lane, N. Y., 1916). *A Hoosier Holiday* (John Lane, N. Y., 1916). *Free and Other Stories* (Boni & Liveright, N. Y., 1918): New York, 1925 (Modern Library reprint with an introduction by Sherwood Anderson); Boni & Liveright, N. Y., 1927. *The Hand of the Potter* (Boni & Liveright, N. Y., 1918): New York, 1928 (Modern Library reprint). *Hey Rub-a-Dub-Dub* (Boni & Liveright, N. Y., 1920). *A Book About Myself* (Boni & Liveright, N. Y., 1922): reissued with an introduction as *Newspaper Days*, Boni & Liveright, N. Y., 1931. *The Color of a Great City* (H. Liveright, N. Y., 1923). *An American Tragedy* (Boni & Liveright, N. Y., 1925): Garden City, N. Y., 1926; H. Liveright, N. Y., 1929; Garden City, N. Y., 1934 (Star Books); World Publishing Co., Cleveland, Ohio, 1947, with an introduction by H. L. Mencken. *Moods, Cadenced and Declaimed*, Simon & Schuster, N. Y., 1935. *Chains* (H. Liveright, N. Y., 1927). *Dreiser Looks at Russia* (H. Liveright, N. Y., 1928). *A Gal-*

lery of Women (H. Liveright, N. Y., 1929). *The Aspirant* (1929). *My City* (H. Liveright, N. Y., 1929). *Fine Furniture* (Random House, N. Y., 1930). *Dawn* (H. Liveright, N. Y., 1931). *Tragic America* (H. Liveright, N. Y., 1931). *America Is Worth Saving* (Modern Age Books, N. Y., 1941). *The Bulwark* (Garden City, N. Y., 1946). *The Stoic* (Garden City, N. Y., 1947). Howard Fast has edited *The Best Short Stories of Theodore Dreiser*, World Publishing Co., Cleveland, Ohio, 1947.

BIOGRAPHY

A large collection of primary sources—comprising manuscripts, correspondence, clippings, and first and foreign editions of Dreiser's works—is housed in the University of Pennsylvania Library. Dreiser's *Dawn* (1931), *Newspaper Days* (1931), *A Traveller at Forty* (1913), and *A Hoosier Holiday* (1916) form, in this order, an autobiographical sequence and are indispensable; his papers, "The Irish Section Foreman Who Taught Me How to Live," *Hearst's International Journal*, XLVI, 1924, and "The Early Adventures of Sister Carrie," *Colophon*, Pt. 5, 1931, may also be consulted with profit. Other articles of varying biographical interest are: Edward D. McDonald, "Dreiser Before Sister Carrie," *The Bookman*, LXVII, 1928; "Theodore Dreiser: 'The Prophet,'" *American Literature*, IX, 1937; "Theodore Dreiser Success Monger," by John F. Huth, Jr., *Colophon*, n.s. III, 1938, No. 1; "Success and Dreiser," by Myrta L. Avary, *ibid.*, No. 4; and John F. Huth, Jr., "Dreiser and Success: An Additional Note," *ibid.*, No. 3. Personal impressions of Dreiser are recorded in the articles "Dreiser's Last Year, *The Bulwark* in the Making," *Book Find News*, II, 1946, and "Dreiser's Last Visit to New York," by Marguerite Tjader, *Twice a Year*, XIV-XV, 1946-47; and "My Brother, Theodore," by Edward Dreiser, *Book Find News*, II, 1946. There are two full-length biographies: *Forgotten Frontiers: Dreiser and the Land of the Free*, by Dorothy Dudley, Smith & Haas, New York, 1932, an early fictionalized biography, reissued with errata, new preface, and illustrations as *Dreiser and the Land of the Free*, by Beechhurst Press, 1946; and *Theodore Dreiser, Apostle of Nature*, by Robert H. Elias, Knopf, 1949, a detailed and interpretative life.

CRITICISM

Of early articles on Dreiser the following are of particular importance: "The Dreiser Bugaboo," *Seven Arts*, II, 1917; "Theodore Dreiser," *A Book of Prefaces*, by H. L. Mencken, New York, 1917; "Dreiser Protest," by Ezra Pound, *The Egoist*, Oct., 1916; "The Barbaric Nature of Theodore Dreiser," in *On Contemporary Literature*, by Stuart P. Sherman (a judgment which Sherman revised in "Mr. Dreiser in Tragic Realism," *The Main Stream*, New York, 1927); "The Novels of Theodore Dreiser," *The New Republic*, April 17, 1915, "Desire as Hero," *The New Republic*, Nov. 20, 1915, "The Art of Theodore Dreiser," by Randolph Bourne, in *History of a Literary Radical and Other Essays*, New York, 1920; and Sherwood Anderson's "Apology for Crudity," *The Dial*, Nov. 8, 1917. Critical statements, characteristic of the 1920's, may be found principally in "Theodore Dreiser, Philosopher," by Paul Elmer More, *The Review*, April 17, 1920; "Crime and Punishment," by Joseph Wood Krutch, *The Nation*, Feb. 20, 1926; *Spokesmen* . . . , by Thomas K. Whipple, New York, 1928; and Carl Van Doren, *The American Novel*, New York, 1921, 1940. Representative appraisals of the next decade are "An American Tragedy," by Robert Shafer in Norman Foerster, ed., *Humanism and America*, New York, 1930; "Theodore Dreiser: chief of American Naturalists," by V. L. Parrington, *Main Currents . . .* , III, 1930; "Realist Fiction: Dreiser," in *The Twentieth Century Novel*, by Joseph Warren Beach, New York, 1932; "Arnold Bennett: American Version," by F. R. Leavis in *For Continuity*, Cambridge, 1933; and "Theodore Dreiser," by John Chamberlain, in Malcolm Cowley, ed., *After the Genteel Tradition*, New York, 1936. Among articles appearing in scholarly reviews, "Theodore Dreiser and Painting," by Cyrille Arnavon, *American Literature*, XVIII, 1945, seeks to establish the relationship between Dreiser's fiction and his knowledge of painting; Charles C. Walcutt, "The Three Stages of Theodore Dreiser's Naturalism," PMLA, LV, 1940, examines with some care the development of Dreiser's fiction. Of later evaluations the most important are "Dreiser, An Inconsistent Mechanist," by Eliseo Vivas, *International Journal of Ethics*, XLVIII, 1938; Oscar Cargill's chapter, "Naturalists," in *Intellectual America: Ideas on the March*, New York, 1941; and "Two Educations: Edith Wharton and Theodore Dreiser," by Alfred Kazin in *On Native Grounds*, New York, 1942. "The Decline of Naturalism," by Philip Rahv, in *Image and Idea*, New York, 1949, is a useful simplification of the critical issues. James T. Farrell's spirited essays on Dreiser may be found in *The League of Frightened Philistines*, New York, 1945, and in *Literature and Morality*, New York, 1947. Among the most recent revaluations are "Theodore Dreiser," by Granville Hicks, *American Mercury*, LXII, 1946; "Theodore Dreiser in Retrospect," by John T. Flanagan, *Southwest Review*, XXXI, 1946; and "Theodore Dreiser," by

Robert E. Spiller, in *Literary History of the United States*, vol. II, New York, 1948. "Reality in America," by Lionel Trilling, in *The Liberal Imagination*, New York, 1950, is of the first importance.

General Index

General Index

James, William, 41, 111
Jewett, Sarah Orne, 111
Josephson, *The Robber Barons*, 131

Kearney, Patrick, 215
Kingsley, *The Water Babies*, 14
Krutch, Joseph Wood, 210

labor unions, 218
LaFollette, Robert M., 219
Lane, John, 167, 169
Lasky, Jesse L., 220
Lawson, John Howard, 251
Lawson, Thomas W., *Frenzied Finance*, 129
Lengel, William C., 104-105, 107
Lewis, Sinclair, 104, 187, 221
Lindsay, Vachel, 180
Liveright, Horace, 169, 180, 190, 220
Loeb, *The Mechanistic Conception of Life*, 236
London, Jack, 35-36, 39, 110
Lowell, Amy, 168
Lowell, James Russell, 62
Luks, George, 53, 162

Major, *When Knighthood Was in Flower*, 64
Marden, Orison Swett, 48, 49-50, 133
Marlowe, Christopher, 135
Martyn, labor reporter, 35
Marx, Karl, 222, 251
Masses, 180, 230
Masters, Edgar Lee, 26, 61, 94, 129, 144, 154, 171, 176, 178, 180, 229-30

Spoon River Anthology, 171
Maupassant, Guy de, 111, 188
Maxwell, John, 25
McCord, Peter B., 30-31, 182
McCullagh, Joseph B., 25, 28-30
McEnnis, John T., 25
Melville, Herman, 4, 34, 56, 135, 236, 249
Billy Budd, 204
Pierre, 205
Redburn, 79
Mencken, H. L., 30, 59, 93, 105-107, 109, 111, 113, 122, 123, 127, 144, 159, 160, 167, 177, 178, 179-80, 187, 210, 217, 230, 232
M'lle New York, 46
Molineux, Roland, 95
Mooney, Tom, 219
Moore, *Esther Waters*, 119
More, Paul Elmer, 237
Morgan, J. P., 131
Muldoon, William, 43, 101, 141, 182
Munsey, Frank, 102
Myers, *The History of the Great American Fortunes*, 129, 131, 134, 222

Nathan, George Jean, 179, 213, 225
Nation, 226
National Committee for the Defense of Political Prisoners, 223
Nazism, 225, 226, 227
New Idea Woman's Magazine, 103
New Masses, 222, 226
New York Central, 100-101

· 263 ·

Index of Works

(*With Some Characters Often Mentioned*)

Index of Works